IMAGES
of America

WHEATLAND

The geographic area of focus for this book is East and West Bear River Townships. Wheatland, incorporated in 1874, was laid out from a portion of Johnson's Rancho and is located between Bear River and Dry Creek in the East Bear River Township. Elizabeth School and ranches are shown on this 1879 Thompson and West map, as well as Camp Far West, McCourtney's, Johnson's, and Kempton's Crossings. The site of Melon's Hotel and Graham's Hotel can be seen along the Emigrant Trail. (Courtesy of *History of Yuba County California*, 1879.)

ON THE COVER: This *c.* 1899 photograph shows the two-story depot that occupied the entire west side of Front Street. In addition to handling passengers, trains arrived with supplies destined for gold mining camps, local ranches, and businesses. Cargo of livestock and produce was loaded and shipped to distant destinations. Pictured on a railroad handcart, from left to right, are Tom Absalom, Tom Covington (station agent), Ernest Monson, Arthur Stineman, and Nance Monson. The long loading platform on the back offered a front-row seat to street dances and parades held on Front Street. Rebuilt as a one-story building after the 1903 fire, the depot was razed in the 1960s. (Courtesy of the Stineman family.)

IMAGES
of *America*

WHEATLAND

The Wheatland Historical Society

ARCADIA
PUBLISHING

Copyright © 2009 by the Wheatland Historical Society
ISBN 978-1-5316-4581-6

Published by Arcadia Publishing
Charleston SC, Chicago IL, Portsmouth NH, San Francisco
CA

Library of Congress Catalog Card Number: 2008933330

For all general information contact Arcadia Publishing at:
Telephone 843-853-2070
Fax 843-853-0044
E-mail sales@arcadiapublishing.com
For customer service and orders:
Toll-Free 1-888-313-2665

Visit us on the Internet at www.arcadiapublishing.com

*This book is dedicated to the people of Wheatland, past, present,
and future. You shaped, molded, and will continue
to influence the lives of us all. We are touched and appreciative.*

Wheatland, a quiet little town in Northern California, still retains much of its historic character.
(Courtesy of Meryl Liebra Parker.)

CONTENTS

ACKNOWLEDGMENTS

The authors are indebted to the many people who helped complete this book. This includes the 1973 original members of the Wheatland Historical Society: Price Waltz, Robert Blackford, Juanita Neyens, Helen Stineman, Miriam Griffith, France Peters, and Jim Hudson. The book *Wheatland 1874–1974* was an invaluable reference of the first 100 years of the city of Wheatland.

Thank you to Jack and Richard Steed for their book *The Donner Party Rescue Site*, Peggy Bal for *Pebbles in the Stream*, the Yuba County Library, and other Yuba County historians who contributed to our knowledge of the Wheatland area. We are indebted to Bill Waggershauser, who took people to view Johnson's Crossing, the Johnson adobe, the Burtis Hotel, Cantonment Far West, and Camp Far West Cemetery. Wes Freeman provided knowledge of the area and early history, including that of the Southern Maidu Indians. Dortha Baker was of great value, identifying people in pictures and sharing memories of a past that few remember. Thanks to the community, it is assured that the thousands of photographs they shared will live on in our archives. Thanks to Nancy Nelson, who donated many hours to edit our scribbling.

INTRODUCTION

The earliest known inhabitants of the Wheatland area were the Nisenan (or Southern Maidu) Indians, who lived in the Bear River area from approximately 500 AD through the 1800s. Their homeland extended from the Consumnes River in the south to the Yuba River. Prior to the Maidu, as far back as 2500 BC, the Sierra and its western foothills were home to the Martis Indians.

In 1844, Don Pablo Gutierrez, who worked for John Sutter at the Hock Farm on the Feather River, discovered the signs of gold on Bear Creek (later known as Bear River). He subsequently applied for a land grant of 22,000 acres from Gov. Manuel Micheltorena of Mexico. Sutter used Gutierrez, a Mexican citizen, to relay information to the governor concerning the insurrection taking place against Mexico. Gutierrez was killed on his second trip to see Governor Micheltorena. John Sutter was responsible for distributing the Gutierrez estate. Sutter sold the land grant to William Johnson at auction for $150. Soon after, Johnson took on Sebastian Keyser as a partner in the property. The Emigrant Trail crossed Bear River on Johnson's property, and Johnson's became a way station for travelers on their way to Sutter's Fort.

Johnson built a small adobe and wood structure, and J. L. Burtis built a hotel at that location. In 1847, after leaving Missouri and heading west, Johnson's Rancho was the first settlement an emigrant would reach before completing the westward journey to Sutter's. They passed through Cabbage Patch (renamed Waldo in 1898), Round Tent, Melon's Hotel, Graham's Hotel, McCourtney's Crossing, and Milltown.

On January 17, 1847, two men and five women, the only survivors of the 15-member Forlorn Hope group from the Donner Party, staggered into Johnson's Rancho with the news that emigrants were trapped at Donner Lake. A Native American runner was immediately dispatched to Sutter's Fort, and in just over a week, a party was sent back to rescue the survivors. All 14 of the rescue party returned with 18 of the 21 survivors; three died en route. After resting at Johnson's, the party left for Sutter's Fort and arrived to a welcoming reception in March. Mary Murphy, a survivor of the Donner Party, later married William Johnson. Because Johnson was described as a "drunken sot" who refused to give up his Native American wives, the marriage was annulled within the year. Mary later married Charles J. Covillaud, who, in 1850, named the city of Marysville after her.

James Marshall discovered gold in Coloma in January 1848. Word of the discovery and samples of gold were sent back to Pres. James Polk in Washington via a messenger, Edward Fitzgerald Beale, an American navy lieutenant and later a brigadier general in the California Militia, for whom Camp Beale would later be named. Soon thereafter, gold seekers, profiteers, and men of all trades headed west to the gold fields.

The first settlers to the area came to profit from the mines and streambeds. Merchants, farmers, millers, and winemakers all had a stake in gold. Fred Wortell Sr., who fought in the Mexican War, and J. L. McDonald, who was stationed at Camp Far West in 1849–1850, bought a tavern and a sawmill that was later converted to a gristmill. Fred Wortell also operated a toll bridge and blacksmith shop a half-mile downstream from McCourtney's Crossing on the old Emigrant Trail from Truckee to Vernon. This town became known as Milltown. McCourtney lived in a large home near the crossing, surrounded by fig trees he planted. Claude Chana, with money made from gold mining, purchased a portion of the Thomas Sicard ranch in 1846 on the south side of Bear River, where he planted fruit trees and a vineyard, and began supplying food to the miners.

Cabbage Patch was established by two black entrepreneurs who decided to sell cabbage to the miners. In 1858, Abraham and Ellen Hambleton ran a hotel and blacksmith shop there. It was located on the south side of Dry Creek below Spenceville. Nearby Round Tent was used as a way station by wagon trains on the Emigrant Trail. There were several hotels along the way to Sutter's Fort, including the Melon's, Graham's, and Burtis Hotels. The main river crossings in the area were McCourtney's, Johnson's, and Kempton's Crossings. Bridges built across the river were washed out by floods and rebuilt. The town of Kearney was laid out at Johnson's Crossing and was proposed to be the primary city in Yuba County. Lots were not sold, so the town never developed. Plumas City, located north of Bear Creek on the east side of the Feather River, was another proposed city that never materialized. Marysville became the county seat of Yuba County.

To protect the emigrants and local miners from "hostile Indians," the army dispatched Lt. George Horatio Derby to determine where to locate a western outpost. The area just east of Johnson's Crossing was selected by Derby for the post, Cantonment Far West, or Camp Far West. Maintaining soldiers at Camp Far West was a problem for their commander, Capt. Hannibal Day, because many deserted to the mines, earning more prospecting than they could as soldiers. The site selected for Camp Far West by Derby was in a strategic position to support the emigrants' journey. It existed from 1849 to 1852, when it was determined the local friendly Maidu were not a threat to the wagon trains or the miners.

During the 1850s, many early settlers to the Wheatland area started farms and families. Some of these families, their houses, businesses, churches, organizations, and schools are depicted on the following pages. The city of Wheatland was laid out by George Holland under the direction of Col. Charles Lincoln Wilson in 1866 and was incorporated in 1874. The new railroad, completed in 1866, ran through the center of town. Wheatland became the primary shipping point for wheat, hops, potatoes, barley, lumber, mining supplies, and copper cement from the Spenceville Copper Mine. In 1878, more than 18 million pounds of various local products were shipped by rail or wagon from Wheatland.

The runoff from the mines and the use of hydraulic mining in Nevada County became a major problem for local farmers. Bear River's main channel relocated three times from 1850 to 1870. Local flooding caused by the runoff eroded fertile soil, washed out bridges, and blocked shipping lanes. The salmon runs up Bear River, a source of food for the Maidu, ceased, and early burials in Kempton Cemetery were covered over by mining debris. It is estimated that 1.5 billion cubic yards of earth, equivalent to more than eight times the soil removed in the building of the Panama Canal, were washed down the Yuba and Bear Rivers from Nevada County. Navigation on the rivers to supply and ship from the mines was impossible. A lawsuit was filed by James Keyes on behalf of local farmers to ban hydraulic mining in California. The lawsuit succeeded, and hydraulic mining was finally banned in California on January 7, 1884, by Judge Lorenzo Sawyer.

At the Durst Brothers Hop Ranch, a labor riot occurred on August 3, 1913. At harvest time, approximately 2,500 to 4,000 migrant workers were brought to the area to harvest hops. The International Workers of the World (IWW) sent Richard "Blackie" Ford and Herman Suhr from Chicago to organize the hop pickers to protest their poor working and living conditions. Ford and Suhr sent a list of grievances to Durst Brothers. On August 1, Ralph Durst formed a committee to address these grievances, and on August 3, an offer to improve conditions was sent to the workers. In response to the Durst proposal, and agitated by the urging of Ford and Suhr, the workers gathered in front of Burdick's Barber Shop to head out to confront Durst Brothers and to reject the offer. When they arrived at the ranch, Ford gave a speech to the workers. Deputies showed up to arrest Ford, but the workers attempted to protect him. Fighting broke out, and a deputy fired shots into the air to regain order. Several more shots followed, and before the melee ended, four people were dead, including county district attorney E. T. Manwell from Wheatland, Deputy Sheriff Eugene Reardon, and two migrant workers. The next day, Gov. Hiram Johnson sent 200 National Guard troops to Wheatland to restore order. Ford and Suhr were charged and convicted of second-degree murder and sentenced to life imprisonment at Folsom. Ford and Suhr had not fired the shots and appealed to the governor for a pardon. After the convictions, among other acts against local farmers, the IWW-led workers retaliated by setting fires to local crops and nailing copper spikes into fruit trees. The governor denied the pardons because the cost of destruction against the farmers of California was so horrific.

Three major fires occurring in 1880, 1898, and 1903 destroyed major parts of downtown Wheatland. The area surrounding Wheatland also suffered from regular flooding. In 1878, Bear River Levee District No. One was formed, and levees were built to protect the surrounding properties and structures. A dam was built in the 1920s to help prevent flooding and to provide irrigation to local farms. That dam was later enlarged and now forms Camp Far West Lake. During the floods of 1955, 1986, and 1997, the military forces from Beale helped maintain the levees in Yuba and Sutter Counties.

Immigrants played an important part in the life and history of Wheatland. In the first major wave, the forty-niners came for the gold. Next came the profiteers and merchants, followed by Chinese, who came to help build the railroad. An enclave of Russian immigrants came to the Wheatland and Sheridan areas to escape religious and personal oppression from the Russian Bolshevik revolution. Driven by the Depression and dust bowl conditions of the 1930s, thousands of emigrants from Kansas, Nebraska, Texas, Oklahoma, and Arkansas made the difficult journey to California looking for work and a better life.

Around 1942, during World War II, another migration occurred when the government opened Camp Beale, an army post northeast of Wheatland. The government bought 87,000 acres from local farmers, telling them that at the end of the war they could buy back their property at the price paid by the government. The U.S. Army used the abandoned towns of Spenceville and Waldo as training and target practice areas, destroying historic remnants of the past 100 years. In addition to housing German prisoners of war, Camp Beale served as the main location for a series of satellite POW camps around Northern California. After the war ended, the property was not sold back to the farmers and ranchers as agreed. Instead, Camp Beale was converted into Beale Air Force Base and was made home to B-52 bombers, stealth SR-71, U-2, Global Hawk, and the support base for the locally installed Titan missiles.

Wheatland maintained its small-town feeling through the 20th century. Many of the original settlers' descendants still live in the area. The cities of Sacramento, Roseville, and Lincoln spread north toward Wheatland, bringing modern congestion. New homes in Linda, Marysville, and Yuba City encroach southward. Developers plan to add major suburban housing and other development to the area. Challenges to the rural life continue, but with luck, the area will not lose the history and feel of this wonderful small town.

One

THE TOWN

Because of its location near the junction of Placer, Nevada, Yuba, and Sutter Counties, the Wheatland area was initially known as Four Corners. In 1866, the city of Wheatland was laid out according to a planned railroad expansion. That same year, the post office was established and the railroad through town was completed. In April 1874, initiated by residents as a way to provide fire protection and enforce sanitary regulations, the city was incorporated. A justice of the peace was appointed, and Wheatland's first official volunteer fire department, the Wheatland Hook and Ladder Company, was formed.

The Chinese, who originally came to Wheatland to build the railroads, were estimated to comprise nearly a third of the city's population in 1878. Anti-Chinese sentiment grew, and local groups worked to remove the Chinese from the area. In 1888, Edward P. Duplex, owner and operator of a barbershop and bathhouse on Main Street, became mayor. He was one of the first black mayors west of the Mississippi and a tireless fighter for African American civil rights. The town grew to approximately 1,000 residents by the year 1900.

In the early years, city services included maintenance for its dirt streets. Until 1901, when electric power was available, a night watchman's duties included lighting the coal oil streetlamps. Water for the city was pumped from underground wells. The city water tower, still the most visible landmark in town, was originally constructed around 1920.

Today the city is planning for growth and working to address the increasing needs of the community. Many fifth- and sixth-generation natives still live in town, but the days when people knew virtually everyone in town are past.

Wheatland is shown looking west from the Masonic Temple on Front Street. The railroad was the lifeline and hub of the community, and the center of the main business district. The depot was a gathering place for socializing and served as the telegraph office. The railroad agent sold fresh seafood sent daily from San Francisco packed in ice. A steam locomotive can be seen on

tracks visible in the photograph. Pictured from left to right are the Carney Hotel, Roddan home (with turret), and Roddan lumberyard. The town and surrounding farmland can be seen in the distance. (Courtesy of the Oliver-Bookholtz family in memory of Miriam Griffith.)

People are seen leaving town after the August 3, 1913, hop riot. In the background, the Wheatland Opera House (Muck Hall) served as a hotel, dining hall, skating rink, dance hall, a theater for stage productions and silent movies, and as a lecture hall. It blew down during the "big wind" in 1938. (Courtesy of Yuba County Library.)

During Prohibition, local farmers began raising other crops such as peaches on their ranches instead of hops. At one time, there was one railroad track with four sidings going through Wheatland. These sidings were used to load and unload products. This photograph from 1938 shows workers taking a break. From left to right are Stan Betterton, Tony Starr, Fred Bogdanoff, and Alan Glenn. (Courtesy of Bogdanoff family.)

MAIN STREET, WHEATLAND, CAL.

A corner of the train depot can be seen to the left of this c. 1915 view looking east down Main Street. Rail lines are visible across the dirt street. Canvas shades have been rolled down on some of the stores. Note the horse and wagon tied up at C. R. Beilby's store on the right, whose sign advertises "Furnishings, Dry Goods, Clothing, Shoes, Hats, Caps, Notions." (Courtesy of Pat Camarena.)

The Masonic Temple, formerly the Odd Fellows Hall, was the tallest building in town. It still stands on the corner of Front and Fourth Streets; the meeting hall is upstairs, and businesses are housed downstairs. Built in 1880, it burned in 1898 but was untouched by subsequent fires. Its brick-walled cellar is the largest in the business district. (Courtesy of Beilby family.)

Some of Wheatland's streets and buildings remain virtually unchanged since the 1890s. These two photographs display similar views of Front Street taken a half-century apart. The photograph above shows how close the business district is to the depot. The modes of transportation shown below have changed, and plaster has been added to modernize storefronts. Seen on the Front Street block, from left to right, are Anderson's, Hudson's, the Bank of America, Muck's Place, Moore Theater, an unidentified business with the depot cart in front, the post office, and Burchell's Appliance Store. Just visible at the far end on Fourth Street are Ed and Bill's Place to the left of the telephone pole and the Elwood Hotel to the right. (Above, courtesy of the Beilby family; below, courtesy of the Kuster family.)

The Chinese community known as Chinatown contained houses, a laundry, a gambling house, and various stores. The Chinese also mined gold and worked on farms, in restaurants, and in homes. First located on Third Street west of the tracks, Chinatown was destroyed by fire in 1898. Rebuilt on the other side of the tracks on Second Street, Chinatown had all but disappeared by World War I. Few photographs of this area exist today. Above is the lower China garden located at the south end of town, around 1909. Few Chinese are buried in the local cemetery because their bones were typically returned to China. Below is a photograph of two young girls, an unidentified child of Chinese descent (left) and Rachael Muck Wilson, playing together. (Above, courtesy of the Beilby family; below, courtesy of Nancy Wilson Tarrant.)

Wheatland's city hall at 313 Main Street, adjacent to the fire department, is more than 100 years old. Originally two stories with a bell cupola, it housed the jail on the first floor with the courtroom above. When the second story burned, it was not replaced. The fire bell, now displayed in front, was then mounted on the water tower to continue as the fire alarm. (Courtesy of Pat Camarena.)

Horse-drawn vehicles had to splash through muddy streets. Wooden sidewalks existed only in front of businesses. Until the city streets were paved, they were watered to keep the dust down. Frank Stineman can be seen on the city water wagon in front of Roddan's lumberyard. Children delighted in rolling up their pants or lifting their skirts and running along behind. (Courtesy of the Stineman family.)

18

Looking south from what is now Nichols Road, this photograph shows Wheatland's rural setting. From left to right are the Wheatland Grammar School, the old water tower, and the three-story wooden water tank building. This red building had two tin tanks on the top floor, another on the second floor, and storage tanks on the ground floor. (Courtesy of the Beilby family.)

Lloyd "Twisty" Harrison was the city engineer for many years. He had only one leg and dug sewer mains, water lines, and cemetery plots by hopping onto a shovel. Pictured in 1943, from left to right, are his wife, Sally (Cook) Harrison, son Stephen Harrison (leaving for war), and Twisty Harrison. Sally, the elementary school cook for many years, was known by the students as "Aunt Sally." (Courtesy of the Harrison family.)

Little is known about the early history of the Wheatland Police Department, and photographs are rare. The city created the position of police judge in 1878, and two men were elected to serve as justice of the peace. The 15-mile-per-hour speed limit set in 1914 had to be enforced, as well as the prohibition of alcohol in 1912. Pictured above is Sheriff Tom Bowser at the Fourth of July parade in 1914. A portion of the present-day police department's collection of artifacts is pictured at left. The patch at the bottom is the oldest. Badges are displayed in the center row. (Above, courtesy of the Blanche Jory Muck family; below, courtesy of Bob Camarena.)

An organized volunteer fire department was formed shortly after the city incorporated in 1874. This independent Wheatland Hook and Ladder Company was outfitted by the city. When devastating fires destroyed most of the town in 1898 and again in 1903, lack of equipment and an inadequate water supply were considered to be major factors. The fire department continues to operate primarily on a volunteer basis and is one of the oldest still in existence in California. Wheatland was only two to three blocks in any direction, so the hand-drawn hose cart pictured above was used until 1949. The department's first motorized vehicle is shown below. New when purchased in 1949, this hook and ladder is referred to as Engine 1 or "Old 411." (Above, courtesy of Bob Camarena; below, courtesy of the Wheatland Fire Department.)

The c. 1910 photograph above on Main Street shows, from left to right, unidentified, Art Stineman, and Mary Stineman. The water tower and grammar school are in the background. A buggy is shown below around 1915 in high water near Wheatland. Dr. Amos Ellsworth wrote, "One held to a straight course between the fences by keeping known landmarks in line." (Above, courtesy of the Stineman family; below, courtesy of Bill Yake and the estate of Dr. Amos Dolbier Ellsworth.)

Two

BUSINESSES, BUILDINGS, AND PEOPLE

The earliest businesses in the Wheatland area were located along the Emigrant Trail near the settlements of Waldo, McCourtney's Crossing, Johnson's Crossing, and Kempton's Crossing. Beginning with a saloon, the first businesses in town were constructed in 1866. When the town was formally laid out later the same year, the saloon was moved opposite the train depot. By the end of 1866, Ziegenbein and Company, E. W. Sheets's blacksmith shop, and Asa Raymond's hotel were also open for business. In *History of Yuba County California* by Thompson and West (1879), it was written:

> Wheatland at the present time has a railroad depot, freight warehouse and water house, four warehouses, one flour mill, one winery, one lumber yard, four saloons, two dry goods and grocery stores, one grocery store, one furniture store, one hardware store, one drug store, one variety store, one millinery, one dressmaking establishment, one meat market, two harness shops, three blacksmith and wagon shops, three carpenter shops, one paint shop, one shoemaker shop, one barber shop, three hotels, one livery stable, one bank, one newspaper, three physicians, one lawyer, a postoffice, one Wells, Fargo & Co.'s Express Office. The buildings may be classified as four brick buildings, thirty-seven other business buildings, one city hall, one Odd Fellows' hall, three churches, one school house, and about eighty dwelling houses.

With the major fires of 1880, 1898, and 1903, most of these buildings were destroyed. Although many establishments have come and gone, the Duplex Barber Shop and Bill's Place were the oldest continuously running businesses in Wheatland. The charming false-front architecture typical of Western structures is still visible in the business district.

Warehouses were located on either side of the railroad tracks. Pictured from left to right are Ben Thomas, Cyrus Harry Dam, Arthur Stineman, and unidentified in the office of Cyrus Harry Dam's warehouse. Also visible in this c. 1915 photograph are a spittoon under the counter, a potbellied stove, and a crank telephone on the wall in the right corner. (Courtesy of the Stineman family.)

The original two-story building at 419 Fourth Street was one of the earliest in town. It had a dry-goods store downstairs and a Woodsmen's hall upstairs. Known as the Wheatland Rochdale Company, a grocery and general purpose store, it was rebuilt after the fire of 1898. Three barrels of vinegar were used to save it from the 1903 fire, and the building still stands today. (Courtesy of the Beilby family.)

Originally a saloon, the Harding Building housed a number of businesses over the years. Pictured around 1917 are Kenneth Latta (left) and Wallace Latta holding pool cues in front of their ice cream parlor. Though it is now known as Bill's Place, the exterior entry tile still displays the name "Harding's." Dynamite was used in the hard earth to help excavate the small cellar. (Courtesy of the Stineman family.)

The interior of the Harding building is shown in March 1926. After Prohibition ended, Bill Hollingshead and Ed Lee purchased the building in the mid-1930s with their World War I bonus money. Then known as Ed and Bill's Place, the bar was renamed Bill's Place after Ed Lee's death. (Courtesy of the Kuster family.)

There were a number of hotels throughout the years in Wheatland. Often renamed by new proprietors, they were used by a wide variety of people from traveling salesmen to local schoolteachers. The Bray Building hotel at 411 Fourth Street burned down in 1898. Rebuilt as the Capitol Hotel, it was later renamed the Elwood Hotel, as pictured above. It was last known as Hotel Wheatland. (Courtesy of Marilyn Waltz.)

The Elwood Hotel's ground floor held a large center lobby. Other businesses, including a dentist, doctor, and barbershop, were on either side. Hotel rooms and a ballroom were upstairs. It survived the 1903 fire when the owner paid men $10 each to help him fight flames from the roof. Pictured around 1914 at the desk are, from left to right, George "Sheepy" Muck, Jane Bowers, and Thelma Harding. (Courtesy of the Handschumacher family.)

Located at 500 Fourth Street facing the railroad tracks, the Carney Hotel had a dining room behind its saloon. The railroad agent notified the hotel of the train crew's arrival time so the dining room could be readied. Dinner was 25¢, including a cigar on the house. The hotel later served as a bus stop, and tickets were sold in the saloon. (Courtesy of the Goforth family.)

The American Hotel was purchased by W. J. Carney in 1886. It escaped the fire of 1898 but burned in 1903. It was renamed the Carney Hotel when rebuilt after the 1903 fire. It continued to be operated by the Carney family, along with the Wheatland (Elwood) Hotel, until both closed in 1957. An advertisement for steam beer can be seen to the right. (Courtesy of the Goforth family.)

The Odd Fellows Hall (left) and Farmers Bank next door were the only buildings on Front Street to survive the fire of 1903. The hall's reconstruction date of 1899, following the 1898 fire, is still visible at the back of the building. Other original details on the first floor are door handles, high ceilings, and windows. (Courtesy of Grace Episcopal Church.)

The Wheatland telephone exchange, one of the oldest in California, was established in 1893. By 1907, it had moved to Anderson's corner stationery store in the Odd Fellows building, where it remained until 1948. The Andersons, including daughter Minnie (pictured), ran the telephone service as a family business. (Courtesy of the Beilby family.)

This business was located on the right side of the ground floor in the Odd Fellows building shown on page 28. Pictured are George Muck (left) and owner Arthur Olsen. It housed a variety of stores, including a grocery, dry goods, drugstore, and clothing shop. The center support posts that once held oil lamps are still in place. (Courtesy of the Blanche Jory Muck family.)

Pictured around 1915 are, from left to right, Wilbur Osborn, unidentified, and Doran Little in front of Wilbur Osborn's store at 410 Front Street. The outline of arched windows and doors is still visible today. When the floor was removed in 1980, rubble from the 1903 fire was between the floor joists. Chinese clay pipes, a notary public seal, melted glass, and a string of brass buttons were found. (Courtesy of Michelle Moore.)

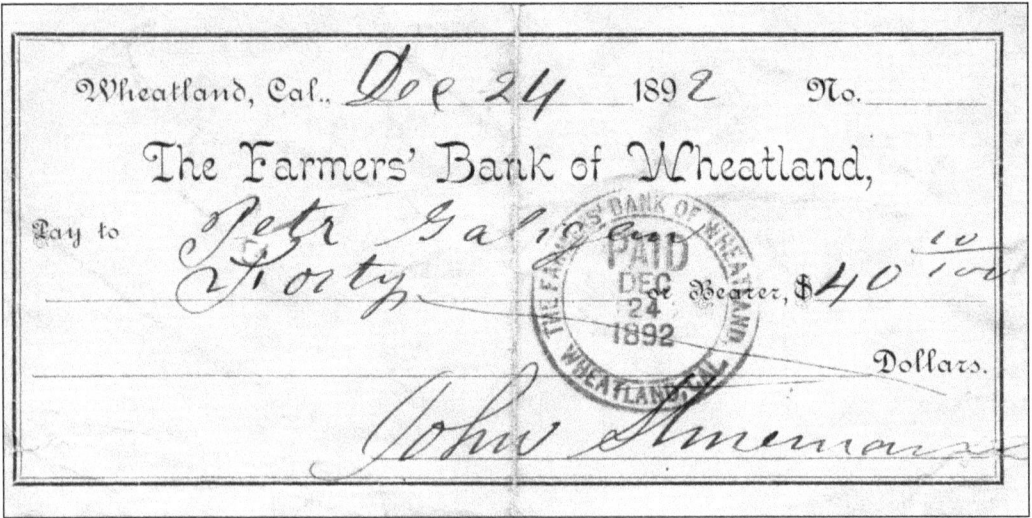

The Farmers Bank of Wheatland was started by local citizens in 1874. Above is an example of a check written by John Stineman in 1892. The bank's fireproof vault saved documents in the fire of 1898 while the rest of the bank was destroyed. Pictured below in 1903 are, from left to right, Lewis McCurry, J. Jasper, E. Langdon, Bill Atkinson, and Dick Sharks. This building at 404 Front Street looks much the same as it did after it was rebuilt. The vault is now used as storage space, and the building's old metal shutters are still on the back windows. (Above, courtesy of the Stineman family; below, courtesy of the Beilby family.)

Originally a two-story wooden structure with an entertainment hall on the second floor, the Stineman building was rebuilt, as shown above, after the 1898 fire. The *Four Corners Newspaper* was upstairs; the McCurry Drug Store and the offices of Dr. C. F. Grant and Dr. Lewis Melton were on the ground floor. Still standing at 420 Front Street, it was reconstructed using the brick walls left standing after the 1903 fire. (Courtesy of Beilby family.)

The first post office was established in 1866 and was housed in a variety of locations. Mail was transported from the depot using a handcart. Located in the one-story Stineman building are the post office (left) and Dr. Amos Ellsworth's office, shown around 1915. The Oakley Tract real estate office is in the Ziegenbein building behind the car. (Courtesy of Bill Yake and the estate of Dr. Amos Dolbier Ellsworth.)

A Fourth of July parade marches down Main Street in the 1914 photograph above. Businesses are, from left to right, Meda Burdick's Agent for the Laundry and Frank Burdick's barbershop behind the car, printing and jewelry repair shops under the arch, and Stagner's Hardware. The pharmacy at 414 Main Street is now a combination of these last three shops (two buildings), with upper brickwork still visible. Pictured at left around 1910, Meda Burdick (third from left) and her friends are in front of the laundry. A boy is exiting the barbershop, where haircuts were 35¢ and shaves 15¢. Charlene (Burdick) Bertolini recalls that while some of the town's dirty laundry was taken care of at her grandmother Meda's business, some was spread as gossip next door in the barbershop. (Above, courtesy of Bill Yake and the estate of Dr. Amos Dolbier Ellsworth; left, courtesy of the Handschumacher family.)

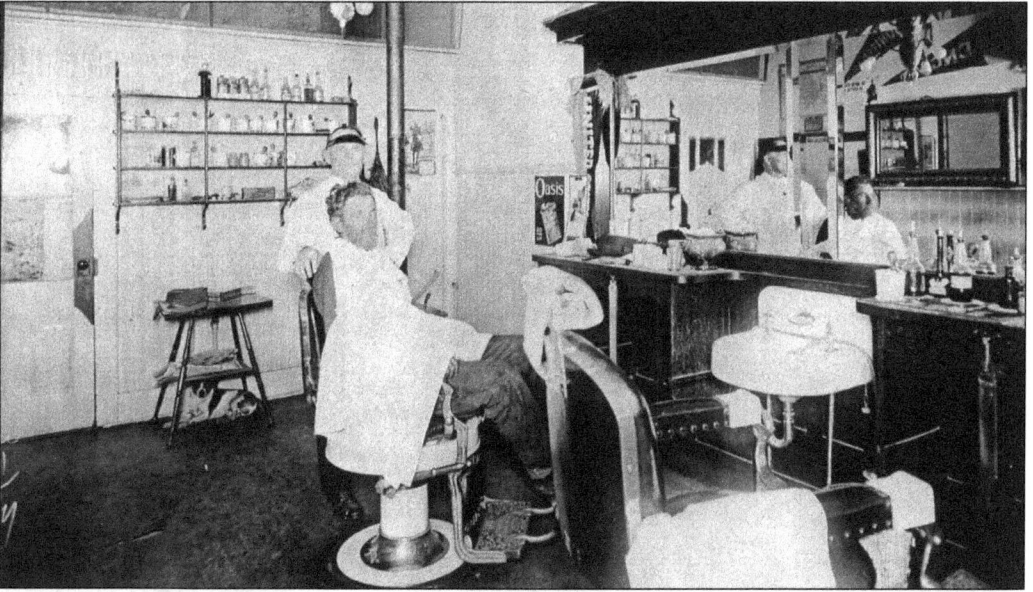

Edward Duplex, one of the first black mayors of a Western city, established Duplex's Barbershop and Bathhouse at 410 Main Street in 1895. This interior view shows it as Burdick's barbershop in 1915. George Handschumacher, the last proprietor, ran George's Barbershop here from 1948 to 1995. At one time, it was Wheatland's oldest operating business, and it appears much as it did in the 1890s and still contains the original potbellied stove. (Courtesy of the Handschumacher family.)

Meda Burdick is pictured in Burdick's Bakery in the early 1900s. This store, located at 408 Main Street, later became the laundry pictured on page 32. These narrow stores had high ceilings and wooden floors. Transom windows above the doors helped circulate air. Many store owners lived behind or above their businesses. The current barbershop includes living quarters that extend behind the barbershop and into what was once the bakery. (Courtesy of the Handschumacher family.)

Claude Muck is pictured behind the counter of Muck's Place at 410 Front Street. This pool hall from the 1930s and 1940s sold beer and had 10¢ pool games. Ice cream and sandwiches were sold from the walk-up window. Claude's son Charles recalled that a man once sat down to visit over a beer and then walked down the street and robbed the bank. (Courtesy of the Muck family.)

An empty field now marks the site of this livery stable on the corner of Main and C Streets. It boarded horses and kept carriages, wagons, and horses for hire. Alfred Griffith often rented to traveling salesmen who arrived by train, headed for foothill communities. His daughter Miriam recalled that no one who returned a horse in less than good condition ever rented from him again. (Courtesy of Beilby family.)

34

The Hicks Brothers' Blacksmith Shop (left) is visible behind hop pickers heading out to the Horst hop fields in September 1906. This shop was on Main Street to the right of the livery stable. Blacksmiths were craftsmen who created and repaired items such as farm machinery and tools, wheel rims, and household objects; they also shoed horses and mules. (Courtesy of the Beilby family.)

Doran Little's blacksmith shop was on Third Street behind what is now Bill's Place. Pictured in the 1890s in the foreground are, from left to right, unidentified, Elmer Roddan, and Doran Little. These shops were constructed of fireproof materials such as brick and corrugated metal. There were three blacksmith shops in Wheatland in 1879. These businesses began to decline with the introduction of the automobile. (Courtesy of Marilyn Waltz.)

As motor vehicles replaced horses, Stephen Hicks and other blacksmiths became the first automobile mechanics. The State Highway Garage in this 1917 photograph was owned by Arthur Phillips. It was located on Main Street next to the railroad tracks, facing State Street. One advertisement listed Dodge and Hudson cars, Holt Caterpillars, and a complete stock of auto supplies and tractor parts. (Courtesy of Elaine Phillips Tarke.)

This photograph, taken from State Street, shows the Wheatland Garage (left) and State Highway Garage on Main Street. The Wheatland Garage building, still standing at 502 Main Street, was once owned by the Beilby and then Nightengale family. In the early 1900s, the state highway included Main and Front Streets. Wheatland businesses suffered when the highway was relocated, making it easier to shop in Marysville. (Courtesy of Elaine Phillips Tarke.)

Three

SCHOOLS, CHURCHES, ORGANIZATIONS, AND EVENTS

The Wheatland School District grew from a series of one-room schoolhouses. Often equipped with little more than a blackboard, a map, and a few textbooks, teachers passed on cultural values along with the "three Rs." Students arrived on foot, on horseback, and in wagons. In 1856, the first classroom was housed in the Roddan family's farm kitchen, west of Wheatland. By 1871, the Wheatland School District was established and a new two-room school erected in town. Over the years, a series of increasingly modern schools were constructed to serve students from Wheatland, Smartsville, Beale Air Force Base, and the surrounding area.

In addition to providing religious and moral guidance, churches reinforced a sense of belonging and provided a community support system. Prior to the building of their church, the first church services in Wheatland were held by the Methodists in 1867. By the 1880s, an additional four churches were constructed (Episcopal, Catholic, Baptist, and First Christian). In 1929, the Molokan Church in nearby Sheridan began serving the Russian community.

Built in 1870 as a Baptist church, Pioneer Memorial Hall has been a community gathering place since its rededication in 1919. Many organizations played a part in the history of the community, including the Civic Club, Masons, Eastern Star, Native Daughters, Scouts, 4-H, and Little League. Town baseball games with neighboring communities became a Sunday pastime through the 1950s. The Wheatland Pet Parade, Memorial Day Luncheon, Fourth of July celebration, and rodeos all were important community events and, with the exception of the rodeos, continue to this day.

Several one-room schoolhouses were located throughout the countryside. One teacher taught up to eight grades in one classroom. Pictured above around 1930 are students in front of Elizabeth School, located at what is now the corner of B and Sixth Streets on Beale Air Force Base. David Creps (second row, center) is shown to the left of his teacher, Velma Louden Hay. He recalls riding his horse to school in good weather. (Courtesy of David Creps.)

In 1871 or 1872, a new one-story, two-room school was erected in Wheatland at a cost of $3,000. The town outgrew the school, located on the south side of Main Street near A Street, by the early 1880s. Rather than remove the expensive bell tower and roof, the entire building was raised up and two new rooms built underneath. (Courtesy of Pat Camarena.)

The eight-room Wheatland Grammar School, on A Street between Main and Olive Streets, was built in 1903 after passage of a $15,000 bond. Public education in Wheatland ended at the eighth grade until 1907, when 23 high school students and two teachers moved into classrooms on the second floor. Elementary grades on the first floor had an indoor playground in the basement. (Courtesy of the Stineman family.)

Amy (Wright) Stineman taught in Wheatland for many years. She is pictured here in 1911 with her first-, second-, and third-grade class at Wheatland Grammar School. When first passing through Wheatland, she thought it would be a dull place to live. She returned in 1911 to teach, met and married Arthur Stineman, and spent the remaining years of her life here. (Courtesy of Dortha Stineman Baker.)

The annual May Day celebration was attended by students and their families. These c. 1910 photographs show this special all-day school event. Pictured above is the maypole dance behind Wheatland Grammar School. A picnic was held north of town in what was then called Dam's Grove. A May queen was elected, and games were played by students, some of whom are pictured below. (Above, courtesy of the Bradshaw family; below, courtesy of Nancy Wilson Tarrant.)

Pictured in 1914 is the Wheatland High School band. From left to right are (first row) Mildred Dam, Frank Sowell, Lizzie Carney, instructor M. A. Kaylor, Thelma Ostrom, and Les Hollingshead; (second row) Lewis McCurry, A. Jolley, Grant Lukensmeyer, Margaret Reichers, Frank Lukensmeyer, R. Koch, ? Miano, and Floyd Muck. (Courtesy of Maryl Liebra Parker.)

High school was taught in the grammar school building until a separate Wheatland Union High School District was formed in 1923. This building, constructed in 1924 at the corner of Olive and Hooper Streets, opened with a faculty of four teachers. Because of the expansion of Beale Air Force Base, it closed in 1961 after a new school was constructed to accommodate student growth. (Courtesy of the Alexander family.)

When the grammar school was condemned as a firetrap in 1934, Eastside Elementary School was erected behind it. After passage of a $33,000 bond, it was built during the Depression by the Works Project Administration. It opened in September 1936 and was considered one of the most modern school buildings in California. Known as Wheatland Elementary, or the "little green school," it closed in 2004. (Courtesy of Chris Bogdanoff Bare.)

Melvin "Gump" Harrison received his eighth-grade Wheatland School report card in 1942. His teacher refused to assign grades for the last three quarters, remarking, "I will fill out this report card when Melvin does something constructive. I can't open up his skull and pour in knowledge." While today's teachers may be tempted, such comments are unlikely to appear on a modern report card. (Courtesy of Harrison family.)

This photograph, taken in January 1913, shows the Elwood Hotel (back left), with Fourth Street running from left to right. The children taking advantage of a rare snowfall are, from left to right, Claude Alexander, Dick Monson, Clyde Waltz, four unidentified, and Henry Sullinger. The barn (back right) displays a painted Chew Mail Pouch tobacco advertisement. (Courtesy of Grace Episcopal Church.)

Mabel Yank, a Wheatland Elementary teacher, began the Pet Parade in 1925. Children, many with dressed-up pets, paraded through town on foot, bike, horseback, or in vehicles or floats. This photograph in front of Wheatland Elementary, taken in the late 1950s, shows a variety of costumes and decorations. This annual May event, still held today, holds many treasured memories for old and young alike. (Courtesy of Grace Episcopal Church.)

Children swam in creeks and rivers and in one of the tin water tanks on the second story of the old wooden water building. Pictured above in the 1930s is the community swimming pool located at 404 Fourth Street. Ethel Luyster, the volunteer overseer, gave teenagers free entry for cleaning the pool. In the water are, from left to right, unidentified, Peggy Luyster and her dog, and Peggy's brother Mick Luyster with their sister Nancy Luyster on his shoulders. In the distant background are the Furneaux house and dairy (left) and the Hicks blacksmith shop. Farm children could often be seen playing in the water. Pictured at left is Dortha (Stineman) Baker cooling off in 1925 in a flood-irrigated orchard. (Above, courtesy of Grace Episcopal Church; below, courtesy of the Stineman family.)

A number of lodges and associations existed over the years, with many succeeding generations participating. The Odd Fellows meeting shown here was held in the Masonic Temple in the 1950s. Pictured from left to right are (first row) Marvin Tull, Earl Goforth, William Bowser, and G. W. Nash; (second row) Marshall Goforth, Wayne Goforth, ? York, and George Handschumacher. (Courtesy of the Goforth family.)

The members of this young women's c. 1896 sewing group are, from left to right, (first row) Annie Stineman and unidentified; (second row) unidentified, Ella Stineman, and Mary Stineman. Note the hats, high-collared dresses, and matching plaid fabric. (Courtesy of the Stineman family.)

The Methodist church, the first church in Wheatland, was constructed in 1870 at 602 Fourth Street. Taken in September 1908, this photograph shows the parsonage to the right, later moved to Highway 65. In 1940, the church became the Assembly of God Church. In the 1990s, a new building was erected with the old church bell displayed in front. (Courtesy of the Beilby family.)

Eber Beilby is shown around 1913 on his way to the Methodist Sunday school. Eber's parents, Ralph and Hattie (Leet) Beilby, ensured that he made a good impression by dressing him in his Sunday knickers. He can be seen carrying apples for his Sunday school teachers. (Courtesy of the Beilby family.)

Russian refugees, many of the Molokan faith, escaped the Bolshevik Revolution and settled in Wheatland in the early 1900s. Standing from left to right are Dorothy (Bogdanoff) Popoff, Hazel (Bolderoff) Bogdanoff, and Andrae Bogdanoff. Andrae's family arrived in 1913 just prior to the Bolshevik Revolution. He donated land for the Russian Molokan Church in Sheridan. (Courtesy of the Bogdanoff family.)

The Grace Episcopal Church, established in 1871 and located at 610 Third Street, has the oldest working church bell in town. The building pictured above, constructed in 1874, cost $1,200. In 1952, a Sunday school room and office were added to the rear. In 2002, the church was expanded and remodeled with the help of church members and a gift from Miriam Griffith's estate. (Courtesy of Grace Episcopal Church.)

The Wheatland Baptist Church was a wooden building constructed in the 1880s at 315 B Street. Destroyed by fire in 1903, it was rebuilt using handmade concrete blocks. In 1929, the Wheatland Civic Club purchased it for $1. In 1957, the Civic Club and the Grace Episcopal Guild transformed the clubhouse into Pioneer Memorial Hall, dedicated to the memory of those who contributed to the community. (Courtesy of Grace Episcopal Church.)

Shown in 1932 at the dedication of the Wheatland Civic Club are the women who helped renovate Pioneer Memorial Hall. They initiated the annual Memorial Day Luncheon because restaurants were not open on Memorial Day when families returned to town to place flowers on graves. Many names of Wheatland-area pioneers are listed on the Pioneer Hall honor wall. (Courtesy of Grace Episcopal Church.)

Fourth of July celebrations included parades, fireworks, picnics, and baseball games. The parades in 1914 and 1915 were especially elaborate, with displays of gaily decorated automobiles and horse-drawn wagon floats. The photograph above shows horse-drawn floats in 1914 on Front Street in front of the depot. Gladys Bever has lasting memories of the parade and recalls that Merle Jasper was crowned queen. Even the smallest entries showed great effort and creativity, as shown below in Grace Phelps's float in the 1913 parade. (Above, courtesy of Gladys Oakley Bever; below, courtesy of Wheatland Historical Society.)

Sunday baseball was a community sport for many years. Town team games were played at Roddan's field at the west end of Fourth Street and later at Wheatland High School. Each small town had its own team that traveled from town to town. These games were well attended and provided an opportunity for family group picnics. (Courtesy of Grace Episcopal Church.)

This town team, the Wheatland Hop Pickers, was made up of local farmers. Pictured in the late 1930s from left to right are (first row) Stan Ferguson and Melvin Baker; (second row) Vernon Baker, Ken Brock, Frank Spencer, Lloyd Cuddeback, and Milton Middleton; (third row) Walt Scheuermann, Allen Glenn, Bill Ball, Bill Peardon, Harold Butler, Bob Blackford, and Walter Smith. (Courtesy of Brock family.)

Erle Hall was designed by Mart Kuster and was built by the families of the Erle District to serve as a gathering place and dance hall. Adah McMillan's Wheatland Band played there every other Saturday night. The band members shown below are, from left to right, Adah McMillan on piano, Willard Jones on saxophone, and Kenneth Brock on drums. The dances started after sunset, and dinner was served downstairs at midnight. The band resumed playing from 1:00 to 2:00 a.m. After that, dancers put $1 in the hat for the band to continue to play. Everyone left by sunup to return to the farms for chores. When the government established Camp Beale, Erle Hall was taken over by the base. (Right, courtesy of Jackie Parker; below, courtesy of the Brock family.)

Hunting was important not only as a sport, but also as varmint control and as a source of food. Pictured above in December 1902 is the Wheatland Hunt Club on Fourth Street in front of the Elwood Hotel. Doran Little is in the foreground at far left, Art Stineman is astride the second horse, William Jasper and his wife, Malinda, are on the balcony above, and ? Taggart is in the buggy. The five duck hunters wearing hip waders are posing below around 1895 with their shotguns and bag limits. Shown from left to right are George Haines (in camouflage reeds), two unidentified, Charles Haines, and John Haines. Charles and John are George's sons. (Above, courtesy of the Stineman family; below, courtesy of the George Haines family.)

By 1911, there were five saloons in town. Beer was only available on tap, so customers could fill up their own pitchers or buckets to take home. Influenced by temperance reform, Wheatland was voted "dry" in the hotly contested 1912 election. Liquor could only be sold by doctor's prescription, so people went to Sheridan for a drink. Pictured here are some Wheatland citizens tapping a beer keg. (Courtesy of Maryl Liebra Parker.)

Rodeos were held for many years in Roddan's field west of Wheatland and later in what is now Nichols Park at the end of C Street. Cotton Rosser provided the stock and portable panels in later years. Pictured here is Bub Sullivan in a saddle bronc event at the last Wheatland Rodeo. These rodeos were discontinued in the 1970s as a result of rising costs. (Courtesy of the Sullivan-Hern family.)

Picnics and family outings were a favorite way of relaxing. Pictured above around 1913 are Lillian Jauch and her mother, Josephine Zgraggen Jauch, visiting Josephine's son Joseph Jauch on his Bear River dairy. One resident recalled that you could travel about three miles an hour by horse and buggy. In the picture at left is the Kuster family on a c. 1917 outing in their Chalmers touring car. Ada Woodruffe Kuster is driving, and her three children—from left to right, Reynolds, Muriel, and Veda Kuster—are sitting on the bumper. Jane Woodroffe Schellenger is sitting next to Ada, and a Mrs. Harkins, who worked for the Kusters as a child-minder and cook, is sitting in the backseat. Sitting next to the lamb is Jane Gilbert Woodruffe with Anna Woodruffe Canning standing on the far right. (Above, courtesy of the Jauch family; left, courtesy of Jackie Parker.)

Four

HISTORIC FAMILIES AND HOMES

There were many families whose homes, farms, and ranches became part of the local history. The original ranching and farming families became a driving force and dictated much of Wheatland's character.

A tour of Wheatland would include some of the homes and buildings in this chapter. Some of these structures are still owned by descendants of the original families. Because names change upon marriage, it may be difficult to identify historical descendants. The surnames may have changed, but after talking with some of the old-timers in town, one would soon find the connection from today's families to those that have been here for 75 to 150 years.

Arthur, the son of Cyrus King and Leoni (Scott) Dam, wanted to marry Annie Stineman, but she was "not in the mood." Determined to marry a Stineman girl, he married Caddie, another daughter of John and Eunice Ann (Browning) Stineman. The marriage lasted 52 years, and they had two daughters—Alice and Elva. Arthur managed the Dam Warehouses and the flour mill along the railroad tracks. He was also an insurance agent. Arthur and Caddie (pictured below) were both active in fraternal organizations. Built as a wedding present in 1903, this home at 309 Fourth Street is still standing and is occupied by Dean and Willie (Lucas) McMillan. (Left, courtesy of the Stineman family; below, courtesy of Elaine Phillips Tarke.)

56

The Daniel Fraser home stood at the east edge of Wheatland. Fraser, born in Nova Scotia, came to this area in 1853. He was a rancher, a founder of Farmers Bank, and a member of the Masons. When the town needed a name, he gazed around at the vast fields of wheat and suggested Wheatland. His home stood until 1948. (Courtesy of Marilyn Waltz.)

After the 1903 fire, John Frederick and Elizabeth (Pinner) Baun rebuilt their home at 401 Fourth Street. Baun, a blacksmith, was highly esteemed by his community. He was a member of the Masons and the Wheatland Fire Department. His home was chosen to be the first home in Wheatland to have the electricity turned on. His sons, David and Fritz, also became blacksmiths. (Courtesy of the Rose family.)

Residence Scene, Wheatland, Cal.

Elmer and Elizabeth (Keyes) Roddan lost their home and lumberyard in the devastating fire of 1898. After the fire, Elmer, a man of immense energy, immediately began planning and ordering lumber to rebuild. Elmer's father, Hugh Roddan, led three wagon trains of pioneers from Iowa to Wheatland. Elizabeth was the daughter of James Haskell Keyes, another prominent pioneer, who led the farmers in their fight against hydraulic mining. Their large two-story house at 505 Fourth Street is now divided into four apartments. Elizabeth Lucretia Keyes and Elmer Ellsworth Roddan, pictured below, were married on January 2, 1889. Their three children were Ottis, Bernice, and Una. (Above, courtesy of Maryl Liebra Parker; below, courtesy of Wheatland Historical Society.)

Dawson and Elizabeth (Chandler) Nichols from Ohio settled in 1854 on a 1,063-acre ranch. Today most of their ranch is in the 11,000-acre Spenceville Wildlife Preserve. Descendants of the family still own 600 acres abutting the preserve, where they operate a camp for children, re-creating life in the 1850s and 1860s. The barn, house, and a few outbuildings can be seen shaded by large oak trees. (Courtesy of Wes Freeman.)

The William and Matilda (Lofton) Creps home was located on Erle Road, west of Dry Creek. In January 1850, Creps sailed around Cape Horn to California. He bought the J. B. Watson ranch, built a large home for his wife, and surrounded it with verandas. The Creps family, pictured from left to right, are (first row) William, Henry, Chester, and Roscoe; (second row) Mima, Letha, and Ella. (Courtesy of Creps family.)

The Miriam Griffith home, located at 601 Main Street, was originally owned by her parents, Alfred and Cynthia (Prather) Griffith. Her father, typical of the men of that era, had numerous professions, including postmaster, hardware clerk, and hop ranch foreman, and he once ran a livery stable. Her mother was a seamstress who stayed with families for a week or two to complete their sewing needs for the year. She was known for the nice touches of lace she added to ladies' clothes. Miriam, an only child, was a longtime resident, a respected teacher in the Wheatland and Auburn schools, and an esteemed historian of the Wheatland community. Miriam is pictured as a young girl in an embroidered dress and elaborate hair bow. (Both, courtesy of Oliver-Bookholtz family in memory of Miriam Griffith.)

In September 1908, the Lewis W. McCurry family is seen standing in front of their home. Pictured from left to right are Lewis W., Florence, Ruby, Belle, Greta, and Lewis M. (killed in World War I). McCurry, the town druggist, had his pharmacy next to Dr. Lewis Melton's office on Front Street. (Courtesy of the Beilby family.)

The Armstead house, located at 609 Third Street, was the home of one of the earliest farmers in Wheatland. In 1853, William Oakley Armstead and Mary (Noe) Armstead farmed 307 acres along Bear River, extending from the city to the river. Armstead signed the petition against hydraulic mining. He donated property, located at the end of Main Street, which became the site of the city baseball diamond and rodeo grounds. (Courtesy of Brock family.)

The John Stineman house at 107 Olive Street was built in 1893. It was a home for his eight children. Lighted with carbide gas, it was the first home in Wheatland with indoor bathrooms. Remodeled in the 1960s to look Spanish, it was returned to its original style by John's great-grandson Robert Stineman in 2007. John Stineman (on the porch) is pictured with his children, from left to right, Frank, Arthur, and Caddie. He served as a supervisor for Yuba County and oversaw the building of the first public works projects in Wheatland—the water tower and water mains. The 1884 Stineman family picture at left shows, from left to right, (first row) Annie; Jack; John; Mary; John's wife, Eunice Ann (Browning); and Caddie; (second row) Ella and Ida. (Both, courtesy of the Stineman family.)

George and Jane (Spencer) Muck came west on a covered wagon from Oquawka, Illinois. Their ranch has been in the Muck family since the early 1850s when George received a land grant. He mined gold for a short time before beginning his farming enterprise. George and Jane operated the Franklin Hotel and, when it burned down, built Muck Hall. In her later years, Jane sat in front of Muck Hall smoking a corncob pipe until someone walked by, at which point she hid the pipe in her skirts. Jane Muck is shown with her daughters-in-law and grandchildren, from left to right, Rachel (Dowane) Muck and her son Bill, Jane Muck, and Califa and George with their mother, Emma (Dowd) Muck. Nancy Wilson Tarrant and Sid Muck, descendants of "Granny Jane," still live on two separate sections of the property. (Both, courtesy of Nancy Wilson Tarrant.)

Francis R. Lofton and Jemima (Harding) Lofton, shown above, came west in five Conestoga wagons filled with goods to sell to the miners. They made a nice profit and were able to grow these funds by taking notes and buying and selling ranch property. Francis became known as the "Illinois Note Shaver." If not paid, he would not hesitate to foreclose. The Loftons had four children: Letitia Jane Harding, Nancy Bradshaw, Matilda Creps, and Albert. The large two-story ranch house pictured below was a stage stop on the road between Grass Valley and Marysville, and was once robbed by Black Bart. One hundred head of horses were used on the ranch, and it had one of the largest red barns in the county. (Above, courtesy of Loretta (Middleton) McClellan; below, courtesy of Irene Creps.)

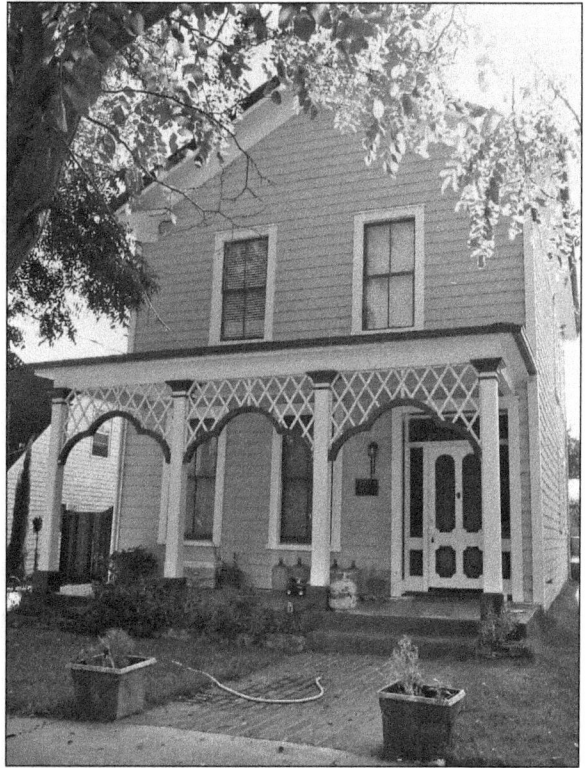

The Holland house, built in 1866 by Crawford Holland, was the first residence in Wheatland and is still occupied today. Pictured below are Raymond Lester Muck and his wife, Blanch (Jory) Muck, who moved into the Holland house in the early 1940s. The Muck house, as it became known, was sold to Dan Risse in 1995. He restored the house to as much of the original construction as possible. A plaque designating it as the first home built in Wheatland was installed by the Native Daughters of the Golden West. (Right, courtesy of Jamie Newman; below, courtesy of the Blanche Jory Muck family.)

The Durst house was built by Dr. Daniel Peter Durst. After he graduated from Jefferson Medical College in Philadelphia, the lure of gold in California beckoned. To go west, he served as a ship's doctor, sailing via Cape Horn and arriving in San Francisco in 1853. He moved to Wheatland in 1867 and purchased 35 acres of land. Shown in the picture, from left to right, are three of Daniel and Rose Frances (Haines) Durst's four sons, Murray, Ralph, and Jonathan. After their father died, Ralph and Murray took over the Durst ranch and operated it as the Durst Brothers. (Both, courtesy of Elaine Phillips Tarke.)

Twins Sherman and Sheridan Harding were born in Nevada City near the end of the Civil War in 1865 to William Harding and Letitia Jane (Lofton) Harding. It was customary for the family to drive cattle up the mountain to the high meadows, where feed was plentiful during the summers. The women often went along to enjoy the cool and pleasant surroundings. Even though not due, Letitia did not make it home in time because the jolting of the wagon brought on an early delivery. Pictured below is the home where Elizabeth (Rich) and Sheridan Harding resided while in Wheatland. (Both, courtesy of Jerna Verrios.)

Purchased by Abraham and Amanda (Jordan) Deck in 1877, this house remained in the family for more than 125 years. The Decks had 13 children but lost four young ones to a fever, two within days of each other. The home still stands at 704 Main Street and looks much the same. This *c.* 1900 photograph shows Amanda Deck in front of the house. (Courtesy of Michelle Moore.)

Elizabeth Hanna Deck lived with her parents until she eloped with Doran Orlando Little in 1896. Doran, a blacksmith whose shop was on Third Street in Wheatland, was killed in 1919 when his Model T stalled on the railroad tracks at the Sheridan crossing. Elizabeth lived until 1957, and both are buried in the Wheatland Cemetery. (Courtesy of Michelle Moore.)

Frances (Scott) and Cyrus King Dam built a two-room house in 1872 on a 3,000-acre ranch adjoining Wheatland. A major addition was built in 1876, including a bathroom with one of the first bathtubs in town. In 1892, it was remodeled into its present form, as shown here in 1899. The home stayed in the family for more than 75 years and still stands at 115 Olive Street. (Courtesy of Elaine Phillips Tarke.)

The Cyrus King Dam family is pictured around 1885. From left to right are (first row) Carrie Gould, Cyrus King, Frances Leoni Scott, and Cora Belk (Carrie's twin); (second row) Francis Herbert, Fannie Charlotte, Cyrus Harry, Etta Pearl, and Arthur King (whose twin, Ella, died in infancy). After his father's death in 1907, Cyrus Harry Dam took over the management of the family ranch and home. (Courtesy of Elaine Phillips Tarke.)

Built in the late 1860s, this was one of the oldest houses in Wheatland when it burned down in the 1990s. It became known as the Ethel Brock Glidden house after the family who purchased it in the early 1900s. The house was on the corner of Fourth Street and Highway 65 and is now the site of a church parking lot. (Courtesy of Brock family.)

Pictured are Ethel and Franklin Brock around 1911. Franklin was a rancher south of Wheatland. They married in 1907 and lived in the home pictured above. After he died in 1949, Ethel continued to live in the house with her second husband, Gene Glidden. (Courtesy of Brock family.)

Five

AGRICULTURE AND MINING

Wheatland's name is derived from one of its main early crops, wheat. As early as 1860, there were 20,000 acres of wheat grown on acreage previously covered with timothy grass and wild oats. In 1849, Claude Chana purchased Theodore Sicard's property on the south side of Bear Creek (now known as Bear River) with money he earned from mining. He planted fruit trees and grapes for wine production and brought in livestock from the south. Chana set up one of the first gristmills, powered by water from Bear Creek.

The areas along Bear Creek were the first to be cultivated, planted, and irrigated. The prairie land was planted in grain and hay where the winter rains provided water. Large cattle and sheep ranches were located in the Erle and Spenceville areas, where the land was less fertile. In addition to wheat, in the 1870s, potatoes, barley, and hay were grown.

Later hops became a significant local crop. In 1906, a special train loaded with 34 boxcars of hops purchased by a buyer from England was shipped out of Wheatland. During Prohibition from 1920 to 1933, hops were replaced with peaches and pears, and a cannery was built. Hop trellises remained in place, and peach trees were planted beneath them.

Almonds did not become an important crop until the 1940s and 1950s. Hops came back after Prohibition but were later replaced by walnuts as the main cash crop in the area. The S. M. Damon Estate purchased the Horst Company property and converted the entire operation to walnuts. They also purchased a large amount of acreage north of Chico, and these two farms became one of the largest walnut producers in the world.

Claude Chana discovered the first gold in this area in Auburn Ravine soon after James Marshall's gold discovery in 1848. Panning proliferated along the Bear River. Chana used money from panning gold to purchase land along the Bear River, where he planted the first vineyards, orchards, and gardens. Claude Chana is depicted in this statue by Dr. Kenneth H. Fox, which stands in Auburn, California. (Courtesy of Richard Paskowitz.)

When the surface gold became scarce, miners formed companies and dug shafts and tunnels to follow gold-laden strata. Charles Cates is pictured (left) with an unidentified miner feeding mules in a rudimentary shelter that also appears to be used for storage. (Courtesy of the Brock family.)

Some miners built small stamp mills to crush rocks containing gold. To extract the gold, miners flushed the crushed rock with water and added mercury. After 1854, hydraulic mining replaced hand digging for gold in many areas. Entire hillsides were washed away with powerful streams of water. Charles Cates, later a farmer near Wheatland, is the person circled in a hydraulic mining camp. (Courtesy of the Brock family.)

The hydraulic slurry was channeled into giant sluice boxes, trapping the gold in riffles at the bottom. The remaining debris, depositing as it flowed downstream, raised creek and river beds. During seasons of high rainfall, the rivers overflowed their banks and spread gravel, sand, and silt on the farmland, ruining it for farming. (Courtesy of Marilyn Waltz.)

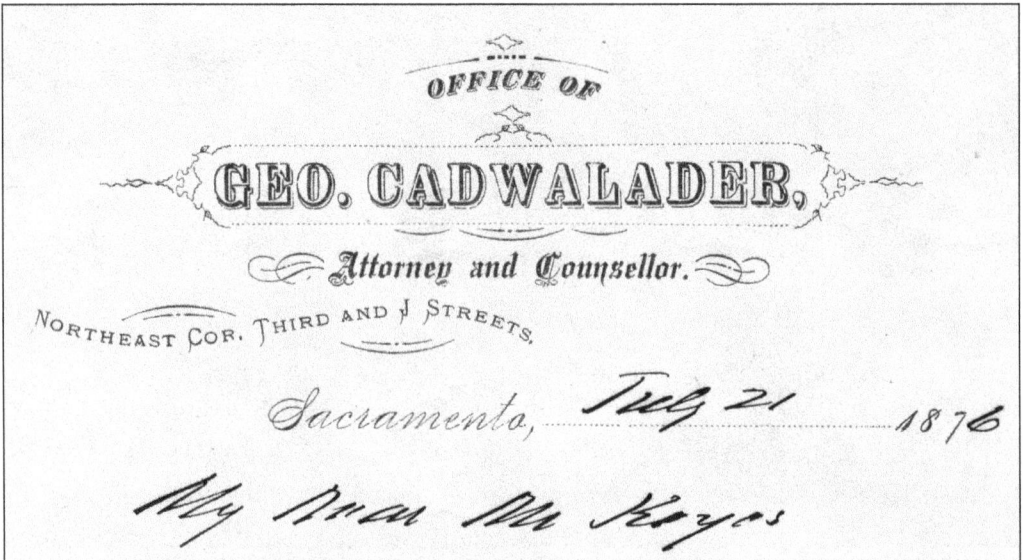

James Haskell Keyes, whose land was near the Bear River, led a group of farmers to stop hydraulic mining. Lawyer George Cadwalader was hired to fight for their cause. This was the first double class action lawsuit in California—the farmers versus the mine owners. The bitter, drawn-out struggle took more than eight years of litigation and ended in 1884 with a ban on hydraulic mining in California. (Courtesy of Wheatland Historical Society.)

Following this ruling, dredging replaced hydraulic mining along the Bear River. The dredger scooped up buckets of rocks, sand, and mud. It then passed over jigs and through amalgamators containing mercury-coated copper plates that captured gold. The stacker carried away the sand and gravel. Today the mountains of tailings that were left behind are currently mined for sand and gravel for all manner of construction. (Courtesy of Library of Congress.)

Dredgers continuously worked the Bear River near the area of Camp Far West. A sprocket for the bucket line of the gold dredger is pictured on a wagon on Front Street between the Masonic Hall and the railroad tracks. The equipment arrived by train and was taken to the dredger east of town. The water tower is also visible. (Courtesy of the Beilby family.)

As depicted in the *1880 History of Nevada County* by Thompson and West, Spenceville was a small copper mining town. Spenceville and the copper mine were chiefly supplied from Wheatland, and the product, copper cement, was shipped by rail from Wheatland. Through commerce, school, and social activities, Wheatland linked the areas of the Erle and Waldo districts, as well as Spenceville. (Courtesy of Nevada County Historical Society.)

This copper mine operated between 1863 and 1918—first for copper, then iron oxide for paint, then sulfuric acid. In 1888, the company was sold to the Imperial Paint Company and Copper Works, which produced the popular Venetian red paint. Unfortunately, it was found to corrode iron nails when barns began to collapse. All mining ceased at the site by 1918. (Courtesy of Nevada County Historical Society.)

Early farming in the Wheatland area began with the cutting of native grasses—timothy and wild oats. Teams are shown mowing hay in the Wheatland area. A team with a 5-foot mower covered half a mile and then rested for 15 minutes. Farms required large numbers of horses and mules to pull various implements. (Courtesy of Tammy Hopkins.)

After hay was cut and raked, it was brought to the stacking area by buck rake and placed on the lift. A counterweight assisted in lifting and maneuvering the load. A horse pulled up the lift by rope and pulley. The load would rotate over the stack. A mechanism would be tripped and the load dumped. (Courtesy of the Don Boom family.)

Men stood on top of the stack to spread the hay. This particular stack of hay is about 200 tons. It was on the ranch of Cyrus King Dam, who at his death owned 2,350 acres and sometimes farmed up to 5,000 acres (some on rented acreage). The Dam ranch had 200 horses and mules. Most of the grain and hay was shipped to large dairies near Los Angeles. (Courtesy of the Don Boom family.)

In the late 1890s, Thomas Earl Akins, with his team of six mules, is delivering a double wagonload of hay to Wheatland. The steeple of the First Christian church can be seen through the trees. Bells are on the hames (collars) of the lead mules to let people know they were coming. Two wagons hooked together made stopping difficult. (Courtesy of the John and Norma Akins family.)

Later on, trucks were used to haul hay. An old Indiana truck with solid rubber tires is shown with a load of hay around 1920. Those standing in front of the truck, from left to right, are unidentified, Paul Simon, Carlos McMillan, and Arthur Stineman. (Courtesy of the Stineman family.)

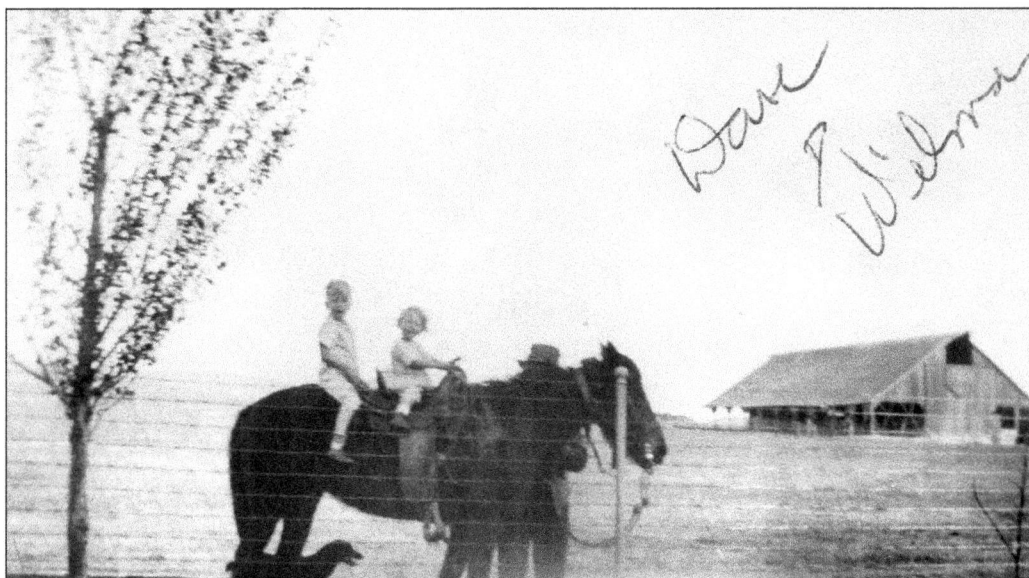

Dave (left) and Wilma Creps are on horseback. Their mother had the yard fenced after the sheep ate the flowers. All the old ranches had big wooden barns for their livestock and feed. Sometimes hay barns were separate buildings, but generally, hay was stored in the top of the barn. A favorite activity for kids was to swing on the barn rope and jump into the loose hay. (Courtesy of the Creps family.)

Horses and mules were used for all manner of activities on the farms and ranches. They were used singly and in pairs for pulling lighter loads and four or more for heavier loads. Pictured is an unidentified man driving a mixed team—a horse and a mule. He is bringing supplies home to the Kuster Ranch. (Courtesy of the Kuster family.)

The first description of a threshing machine was of one used on Claude Chana's farm in 1852. It was a one-horse-power endless-chain thresher used to thresh a crop of barley raised by J. L. Burtis. The first harvesters were stationary. The grain was cut with knives or scythes and was brought to the thresher. Threshers were driven by a belt attached to the flywheel of a steam engine or tractor. This thresher was in operation in Yuba County in 1910. The dry climate enabled farmers

to ship grain by rail without going through a lengthy and expensive drying process. In an 1883 letter to his friend Edward Bovee, J. H. Hammon described Wheatland as "on the Rail Road & the whole country is a solid Wheat field Every Body Raising Wheat for Europe." (Photograph courtesy of Tammy Hopkins; letter courtesy of Chris Bogdanoff Bare.)

An eight-horse team and the plow shaker are taking a break from plowing on the Kuster Ranch. Newly turned soil, barns, and a windmill can be seen. Water was pumped by the windmill into the tank house for use by the family and for the farm. Mules were used to plow and mow from the 1850s until the 1920s. (Courtesy of the Kuster family.)

Five teams of eight horses are shown on the C. K. Dam Ranch. The five teams were staggered slightly, one behind the other, so they would not have to walk on ground that was already plowed. Each team could pull three or four 12-inch plows. Five teams of eight could cut a 24-foot swath. (Courtesy of the Don Boom family.)

This harvesting scene, taken in 1928, shows the harvester being pulled by 30 bald-faced mules. Lawrence "Jack" Bradshaw, father of Marilyn Waltz, stands on the platform. Jack's father, Jefferson Davis Bradshaw, often rode in the outrigger over the wheelers. Donald Boom rode in the outrigger as a boy with a little bucket of small stones used to remind the mules to pay attention. (Courtesy of Marilyn Waltz.)

In the decade from 1910 to 1920, mules were replaced by tractors. This Holt 75 had tracks supporting the main weight of the tractor, which enabled it to travel on uneven ground. A single steel wheel for steering was in front. Awnings were placed on the machinery to shade the men from the summer sun. (Courtesy of Maryl Liebra Parker.)

Harvesters, with their gears and chains, made a great backdrop for photographs. The back of this photograph, taken at the Kuster Ranch in the Erle District, says, "The charming Crew, including Mumps." This harvesting crew of Kuster siblings was, from left to right, (first row) John and Emery; (second row) Sam, Mary Kay (Mumps), and Martin. (Courtesy of the Kuster family.)

Rain-fed grain (wheat) was the basic crop of the region from 1850 to 1890. Other crops were barley, potatoes, beans, corn, and hay. Arthur Phillips Jr. ("Artie") and his dad, Arthur Phillips Sr. (known by everyone as "Flip"), are seen cutting corn at their Erle ranch in 1929. (Courtesy of Elaine Phillips Tarke.)

Crops needing a year-round source of water were planted near creeks and rivers. With the advent of water districts and water wells, orchards like this young peach orchard were planted farther from the river. Checks were ridged up so the trees could be flood-irrigated. This peach orchard, photographed about 1938, was on the Eber Beilby ranch west of town. (Courtesy of the Beilby family.)

Shown in 1938 are two unidentified hired hands (left) sowing a cover crop beneath peach trees while Don Beilby is balancing on the tongue of the wagon. (Courtesy of the Beilby family.)

Problems came with the planting of orchards. Rabbits ate the bark of the young trees, girdling and ultimately killing them. Men from town and the surrounding farms participated in organized rabbit hunts. The rabbits were driven to a rabbit-proof fenced area and killed. This rabbit hunt was on Bear Valley Road, now Bear River Drive, in the 1920s. (Courtesy of the Beilby family.)

Fruit and nut trees need to be sprayed to prevent and treat a variety of problems—from insects to assorted rots. Norton Brock (left) and Ray Beilby are seen resting after spraying the orchard at the side of the Dam house in Wheatland. (Courtesy of the Brock family.)

During harvest season, peach pickers climbed 12-foot ladders, picked the fruit, placed it in canvas sacks strapped over their shoulders, climbed down the ladder, and emptied the fruit into lug boxes, seen at the right. Another crew swamped the peaches, lifting the 50-pound boxes of fruit onto a trailer. High school kids earned money picking, swamping, or irrigating peaches. Arthur Stineman (above) is standing by a ladder in a peach orchard on his Oakley Lane ranch. A peach orchard produces for 20 years. Below, John Stineman can be seen crouched between the tractor and trailer; from left to right (second row) are three unidentified workers and Chester Stineman, seen swamping peaches in the same orchard as pictured above. Bercut-Richards, Schukle, California Packing Corporation, and the Lincoln Cannery were the major canneries that bought peaches from local growers. (Both, courtesy of the Stineman family.)

Almonds grew well. Taken on the C. K. Dam Ranch in 1920, this photograph shows women hulling almonds by hand. By the 1950s, almonds were knocked from the trees with poles and mallets onto canvas sheets and taken to an area where they were hulled. Today the process is all mechanized with shakers, sweepers, pick-up machines, and large hulling machines. (Courtesy of the Don Boom family.)

Orchards were removed when they decreased in productivity, became diseased, or were replaced by a more lucrative crop. This photograph shows a peach orchard on the Stineman ranch being pulled out, cut up, and burned. The Caterpillar tractor is a D-4. (Courtesy of the Stineman family.)

There were stockmen in the Erle, Waldo, and Spenceville areas. Chester Creps is seen on horseback with some of his cattle. The Creps family had 200 to 300 head of cattle and sheep and about 400 acres of grain. Their land along Dry Creek was ideally suited for cattle. They would drive the cattle to the Sutter Bypass for summer feed. (Courtesy of the Creps family.)

Cowboys from the Kuster Ranch take time out for a *c.* 1905 photograph. The Kuster brothers, pictured from left to right, are (first row) Emery; (second row) Martin and Sam. (Courtesy of the Kuster family.)

Marking (castrating) lambs was an early spring occurrence on the Dam Ranch. The lambs were castrated when they were very young. Their tails were bobbed at the same time. Sheep were raised for meat and for wool. (Courtesy of the Blackford family.)

The Blackford, Dam, and Boom families had large herds of sheep that they would drive to their summer camp in Cisco Grove. In the photograph is Harry Dam with his wife, Magdalene (Haines) (second row, sixth and seventh from the left), their daughters, sons-in-law, and grandchildren at their summer camp. Also in the second row is Judd Ridener (far left), visiting from a neighboring camp. (Courtesy of the Blackford family.)

Six

HOPS

From the 1880s on, hops were important to Wheatland. A labor-intensive crop to harvest, hops required up to 4,000 migrant workers coming to town for seasonal work, most arriving by railroad. In 1898, a local post office was located at Horstville, the name given to the company town on the ranch owned by E. Clemens Horst Sr. Horstville had company housing, a dining hall, a tent city for seasonal workers, and a company store where workers could purchase food and dry goods.

After growing various other crops, Dr. Daniel P. Durst, a physician who made Wheatland his home in 1867, began growing hops along Bear River in 1883. Two of his four sons, Ralph and Murray, continued the hop operation as the Durst Brothers after their father's death. In 1913, Durst Brothers advertised for 2,800 workers, but more than 4,000 wanted work. Over 2,000 of the workers were immigrants representing 29 nationalities. The migrant labor unrest, partly agitated by the International Workers of the World (IWW) union representatives, led to the hop riot of August 1913. This riot and the murder trials that followed were known throughout the country and became a textbook case study of labor unionization.

S. S. Steiner, Inc., purchased the Wolf ranch in 1940 and changed the name to the Golden Gate Hop Farm. It was managed by Earl Goforth. In 1957, the ranch was purchased by E. Clemens Horst Jr. Horst also purchased the Durst ranch and changed the name to the Bear River Hop Farm. Smaller operators in the area included the P. C. Drescher and the Gambrinus Hop Ranches.

E. Clemens Horst Sr. invented a mechanized hop picker that revolutionized the harvest process. The Horst family hosted annual meetings of brewers and growers at the ranch. In addition, family members came from San Francisco and used the Durst house for pheasant and deer hunting parties and as an escape from city life. Descendants of the Horst family live in the Durst house today. The only remnants left of the hop era are the deteriorated structures of two former drying kilns just east of the Durst house.

Hop Pickers

Hop Picking will commence on P. C. Drescher Ranch
One Mile East of Wheatland between

August 5th and 10th

High Camping Ground adjoining Hop Fields, Deep Well
of Good Water and Free Wood on Grounds. Grocery,
Bakery and Vegetable Wagons take Orders and deliver Goods twice each day from Town. Mail can be addressed to Ranch and will be delivered twice daily.
Wagon will meet all Trains and Pickers and Baggage
will be transported to and from Ranch free of charge.
The place consists of

105 ACRES

of well cultivated Hops, all on high trellis, good stand
of Hops with no undergrowth and light foliage. Will
pay same as other yards at beginning which will be
not less than

1.00 per 100 Pounds

to all who stay through. We have no interest in any
store or saloon, pickers may patronize whom they please.
Negotiable checks will be given each day good for face
value at office or any store or wagon in field. Limited
number Tents can be had at normal figures. No lay
off after beginning. No undesirable element allowed
on Ground or Field. Send in name to insure job. All
letters answered. Address

Wm. MUCK,

Superintendent Of

P. C. Drescher Ranch

This P. C. Drescher Ranch advertisement is typical of the times. It was a daunting task for a town of 1,000 residents to bring in as many as 4,000 seasonal workers. (Courtesy of Wheatland Historical Society.)

Wagons with teams of horses were used to pick up the hops, transfer them to the kilns, and bring them to market. In the foreground of this picture are 11 horses (including a mule foal in front next to the bicycle rider). In the background, from left to right, are the back side of the Durst home, several hop sheds, outbuildings, and the familiar hop kilns. (Courtesy of the Stineman family.)

These tent cities provided housing to many migrant workers who came to town by rail. Although ranches typically provided tents for a fee, on some ranches, free tents were used as an incentive to attract workers. Looking west into town from the Durst ranch, the Wheatland water tower can be seen in the background. (Courtesy of Maryl Liebra Parker.)

The Horstville store on the Horst ranch sold provisions to the workers. This company store took chits and hard currency. The chits would be deducted from employee wages. It was convenient because most of these migrant workers came to town by rail and had no shopping alternative other than a 3-mile walk to town. (Courtesy of Nancy Wilson Tarrant.)

Workers of all types came for this short-term seasonal work. The couple above may have come from any walk of life. These seasonal jobs were an important source of extra income for families, including locals with their own farms. The job was perfect for teachers who were off for the summer to earn extra money, and they could bring their children along. (Courtesy of the E. Clemens Horst Sr. family.)

Another typical camp scene shows workers preparing meals on an outdoor cooking pit provided by the ranch. This tent city is pitched among the hop vines. In the background, large round tents can be seen to the left above the tents, with a ranch building to the right. (Courtesy of the E. Clemens Horst Sr. family.)

With the family dressed in their finest before going on an outing or to church, this picture was taken in front of a kiln at Horstville above Grasshopper Slough. Families that worked year-round at the ranches usually lived in company housing provided by the hop owners. Horstville had a post office until 1901, and its company store and mess hall were self-sufficient. (Courtesy of Marilyn Waltz.)

Are the children looking for pollywogs, a lost possession, or something else? In the background are the trellises used to grow hops. Grasshopper Slough was in the middle of the Horst Ranch and was a popular spot for recreation or serenity after a long, hot day's work. Respite from the summer heat was much needed at the end of the day, especially for the children. (Courtesy of Nancy Wilson Tarrant.)

The Wellman triplets, from left to right, are Amos, Aaron, and Amy with their mother Ency (Paige) Wellman (far left) during the hop harvest. When they were born on December 2, 1878, triplets were a rarity. For 15¢ apiece or 25¢ a couple (10¢ for children), the triplets could be viewed as "The Greatest Curiosity Now in the State" at the 1879 California State Fair. (Courtesy of Phyllis Smith.)

A typical field scene included workers of all nationalities, sexes, and ages. An account at the time reported 29 nationalities that came to harvest. Long-sleeved shirts and hats were necessary to protect skin from the hot, direct, summer sun. The basket with the Durst label shows where these workers picked hops, and the ticket on the father's hat is the family's picker number to credit wages. (Courtesy of the Oliver-Bookholtz family.)

Below, a picker dragged his bag of picked hops to the weight scale before they were loaded onto the wagon. The weight of the hops picked determined what amount would be credited to the worker's picking account. In later years, hop vines were cut in the fields, loaded directly onto wagons, and the vines hauled to sheds for processing. This change in the harvest process eliminated many laborers. (Courtesy of Tammy Hopkins.)

The scale visible behind the wagon weighed the hops. The wagonload of picked hops was taken to the drying kilns, and if possible, it was driven up to the top platform or pulled up by horse-drawn ropes and pulleys. George Denna Wirts (second from the left) stands next to the white horse at the Durst ranch. (Courtesy of Wheatland Historical Society.)

At the kiln, the hops were unloaded and spread onto burlap mesh drawn over a lattice structure of two-by-twos located at the top of the kiln. The rising hot air heated from wood, oil, or gas dried the hops. Once dried, the hops would be moved to the cooler shed. (Courtesy of the E. Clemens Horst Sr. family.)

Hop pickers originally worked in the fields picking, bagging, and weighing hops. One of the first innovations to the harvesting process was to cut the vines down in the fields and haul them to the hop sheds for processing, thus eliminating many laborers. (Courtesy of the Oliver-Bookholtz family.)

Hops, vines, and leaves were hauled to the hop sheds for processing on wagons drawn by horses, mules, and later tractors. The hop vines then went to the processing sheds to be lifted from the wagons onto the processing area. Cleaned hops were then taken to the kiln for drying. After drying, the hops were put into a cooling storage area and baled prior to shipment. (Courtesy of the Oliver-Bookholtz family.)

Workers are shown in the hop sheds separating the hops from the vines and leaves. The picked hops were then transported to the drying kilns. Picking machines later developed by E. Clemens Horst Sr. further revolutionized this process, decreasing the cost of labor and processing. (Courtesy of the Oliver-Bookholtz family.)

The hops were cleaned by separating them from the vines and leaves. A conveyor belt was the most efficient method of getting the cleaned hops from the hop shed up to the drying level of the kiln. (Courtesy of the Oliver-Bookholtz family.)

In the hop shed bagging station, this worker bagged the cleaned hops from the processing shed prior to having them loaded onto a wagon. A wagon full of these bagged hops was then driven or hauled up to the drying kiln. (Courtesy of Tammy Hopkins.)

This 1912 picture of the hop storage area, or cooler shed, shows inspectors who assessed the quality of the hops prior to purchase. Proper drying was important so the crop would not mildew and spoil during shipment. (Courtesy of Elaine Phillips Tarke.)

The picture shows 200-pound bales of hops being sewn together for shipment. The hops were dropped down a chute and compressed in the bagging machine and then filled, compressed, and filled again to approximately 200 pounds before sewing. (Courtesy of Ginger Horst and Winifred Pike.)

Packed bales are stacked near wagons to be transported to the train station and shipped out of Wheatland to buyers around the world. According to a local newspaper, the largest shipment recorded from Wheatland was 34 boxcars of hops shipped to England in 1906. (Courtesy of the Stineman family.)

Workers with signs are shown outside strike headquarters on Main Street. Richard "Blackie" Ford and Herman Suhr of the International Workers of the World came from Chicago to help organize the hop workers and to assist them in obtaining better wages and working conditions. (Courtesy of Wheatland Historical Society.)

On August 3, 1913, the morning of the Wheatland hop riot, workers gathered to listen to a union speaker. The Durst ranch was located about one mile east of town; several hop kilns can be seen in the right background. Food booths and temporary stores were set up on the left for the seasonal workers. The Durst house can be seen in the center background. (Courtesy of Maryl Liebra Parker.)

The day after the August 3, 1913, riot, Gov. Hiram Johnson ordered militia units from Chico, Woodland, and Sacramento to Wheatland to calm down the agitated workers. In this picture is an armed trooper on duty at the worker's camp. (Courtesy of the E. Clemens Horst Sr. family.)

This picture was taken the day after the riot; people are anxiously waiting for a train to take them out of town. (Courtesy of the Oliver-Bookholtz family.)

Prior to the riot, Yuba County sheriff's deputies were called to maintain order. Fighting broke out, and a deputy fired shots into the air. Chaos ensued, and more shots were fired. Before order was reestablished, six people were injured and four killed. Pictured at right is E. T. Manwell, a Wheatland resident and Yuba County district attorney who was one of those killed. Blackie Ford, Herman Suhr, and two others were charged with murder. Pictured below is Blackie Ford (middle of the backseat) being driven to the courthouse. Ford and Suhr were convicted of second-degree murder and sentenced to life at Folsom Penitentiary. In the following years, the IWW targeted farmers, burning wheat fields and driving copper spikes into fruit trees to cause financial harm. (Right, courtesy of Tammy Hopkins; below, courtesy of Maryl Liebra Parker.)

Pictured next to the car on the Golden Gate Hop Farm are, from left to right, Marshall, Earl (the boys' father), Roger, Wayne, and James Goforth. Earl was the ranch superintendent and operated the ranch for S. S. Steiner. Four drying kilns are shown in the background. (Courtesy of the Goforth family.)

The six tractors shown are on the Durst ranch in front of the drying kilns. Horses were replaced by the Cletrac (Cleveland tractors), and work on the ranch became simpler compared to working with horse teams. It is sad to see an era end, but that is progress. (Courtesy of Nancy Wilson Tarrant.)

Seven

MILITARY HISTORY

During World War II, the government needed an army post for the war effort and chose the acreage northeast of Wheatland as the site. The local farms and ranches in the Erle District were purchased by the government through eminent domain. In honor of Gen. Edward Fitzgerald Beale, the post was named Camp Beale and became operational in 1942.

The post was used for training infantry troops and the 13th Armored Division during World War II. A German prisoner of war camp was established there and housed up to 200 German prisoners. The abandoned communities of Spenceville, Waldo, and Round Tent were used for target practice, wiping out the remaining historic structures from these communities. World War II ended, and the property was not returned to the former owners. In 1948, Camp Beale was converted to Beale Air Force Base and was initially used to train navigators and bombardiers.

In 1960, during the cold war, Beale Air Force Base became home to B-52 long-range bombers. In 1962, it served as a support base for the locally installed Titan missiles in Lincoln, the Sutter Buttes, and Chico. In 1965, it became home to the SR-71 Blackbird and U-2 reconnaissance airplanes. This mission was the core of the motto of the base, "In God We Trust, All Others We Monitor." The base then became home for the PAVE PAWS radar program that served to track satellites and provide early warning for missiles launched against the West Coast of the United States. The "defense through knowledge" function of the base was expanded and improved with the arrival of the R-Q Global Hawk in 1999, a high-altitude, long-endurance, and unmanned reconnaissance aircraft.

With the build-up of Beale Air Force Base and the military population, the Wheatland school system was significantly impacted and eventually tripled in size. Today the base melds comfortably into the community of Wheatland as well as Yuba County.

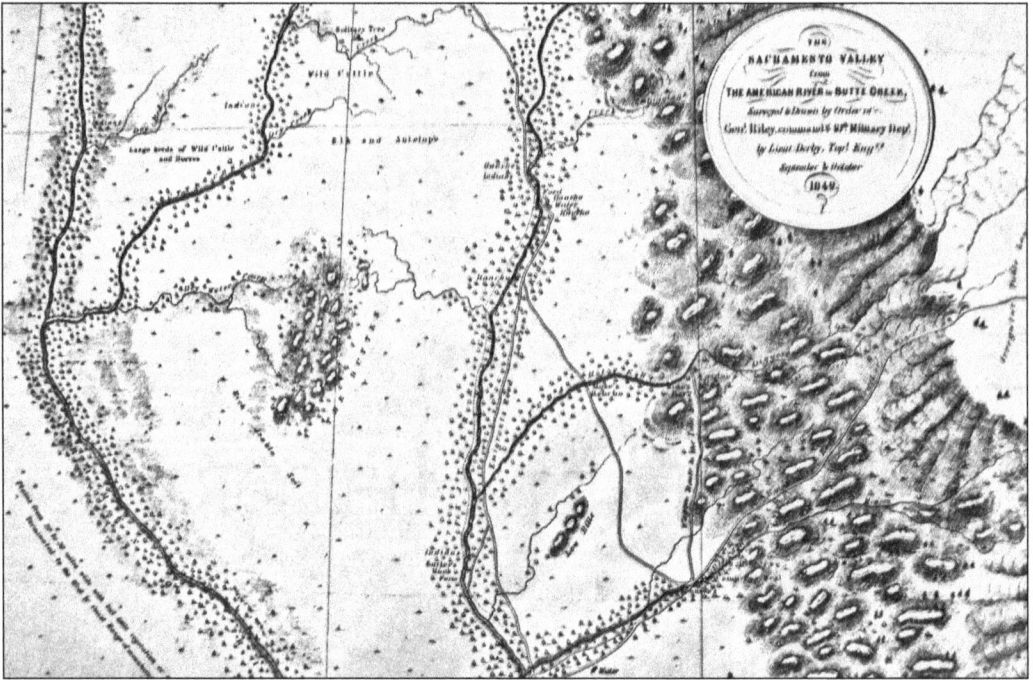

In 1849, the Sacramento Valley was surveyed by Lt. George Derby, who was commissioned to find a suitable military outpost to protect the miners and emigrants from Native Americans. The survey included Feather River, Sacramento River, and Bear Creek. Because it was thought to be less subject to disease and was more accessible to Sutter's Fort and the mining areas, the Bear Creek site (Johnson's Crossing) was chosen. (Courtesy of Jack Steed.)

Lt. George Horatio Derby surveyed the Sacramento Valley and Camp Far West specifically. This Mexican War hero became better known under the pseudonyms of "John Phoenix" and "Squibob," the humorist of the Gold Rush era. His articles first appeared in the San Francisco Herald and San Diego Herald newspapers. (Courtesy of Bancroft Library.)

This is a photograph of a painting by Frederich G. Dowane of Wheatland. The painting depicts Camp Far West in 1849. The painting was presented at the California Exposition in 1886 and was at Sutter's Fort until 1977. (Courtesy of California State Parks, 2008.)

Hannibal Day, captain of the U.S. Army 2nd Infantry, was the commander of Camp Far West. His reports described the conditions at the cantonment and the desertions of his troops to the gold mining areas. During the Civil War, he became a general. (Courtesy of Jack Steed.)

Robert Murray was the first military surgeon at Camp Far West. He became surgeon for the Presidio in San Francisco and eventually the surgeon general of the U.S. Army. (Courtesy of Library of Congress.)

Stephen J. Fields of Marysville was a young attorney and the first alcalde (mayor) having judicial powers. In 1850, with the founding of Marysville, he proposed that the soldiers at Camp Far West be used to keep order. At the time, Marysville had no law enforcement agency. (Courtesy of Library of Congress.)

This marker depicts the Camp Far West outpost from 1849 to 1852. A military presence was later reestablished when Camp Beale opened in October 1942, and Beale Air Force Base opened in 1948. (Courtesy of Richard Paskowitz.)

Camp Beale was opened in 1942 during World War II to serve as a training camp for the 13th Armored Division. The site, just north of Camp Far West, displaced farmers whose land was purchased by the U.S. government. Beale was named after Edward Beale, the man who informed Washington, D.C., that gold had been discovered in California in 1848. (Courtesy of Beale Air Force Base.)

Tanks, artillery, and aircraft were used at Camp Beale to simulate attacks on the fictional German town of Spenceburg, the real pioneer town of Spenceville. (Courtesy of Beale Air Force Base.)

Rodeos offered recreation to the soldiers stationed at Camp Beale. The animal stock was supplied by local Wheatland ranchers. The rodeo arena still exists, and Beale Air Force Base is one of the few bases where horses can be boarded. (Courtesy of Beale Air Force Base.)

Camp Beale also served as a German prisoner of war camp. German prisoners peeled potatoes, grew their own food, and helped maintain the infrastructure at Camp Beale. Due to their efforts, there was a reported savings of millions of dollars. (Courtesy of Beale Air Force Base.)

The German stockade is the only standing remnant left of the prisoner of war camp. The bleak concrete structure contains drawings by the prisoners. (Courtesy of Beale Air Force Base.)

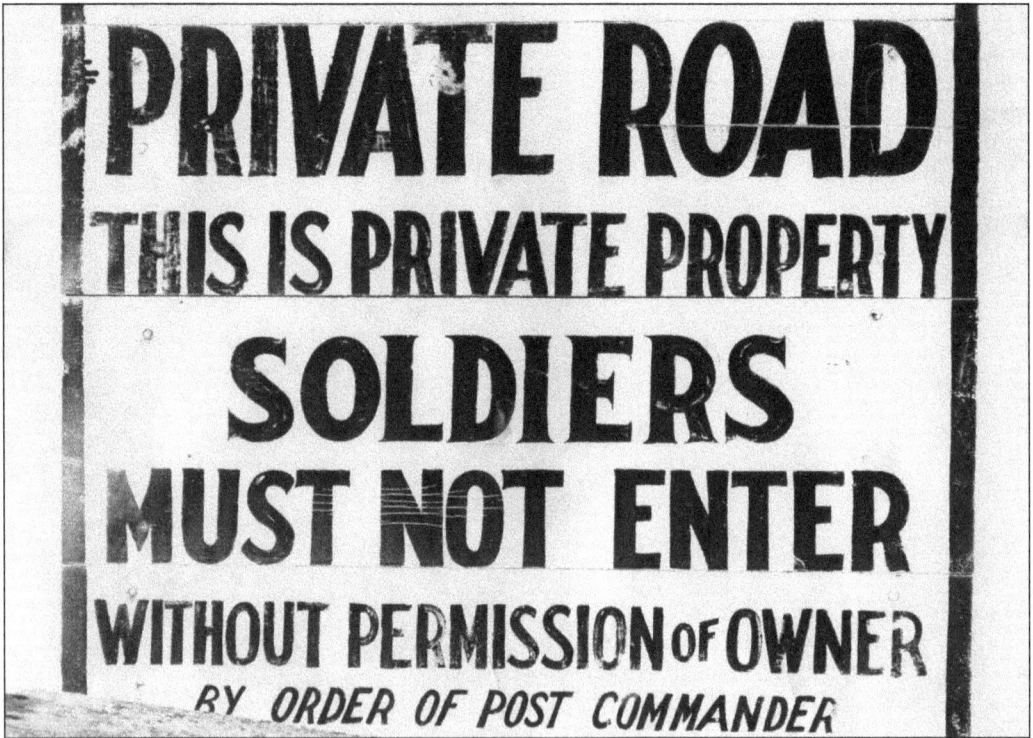

PRIVATE ROAD
THIS IS PRIVATE PROPERTY
SOLDIERS
MUST NOT ENTER
WITHOUT PERMISSION of OWNER
BY ORDER OF POST COMMANDER

There were signs that all was not well between the military and the displaced farmers of Wheatland. This ill will was extended when the farmers' properties were not sold back to them after World War II. Camp Beale was downsized and then became Beale Air Force Base. Under the direction of Beale personnel, Titan missile facilities were erected in the Sutter Buttes, Chico, and Lincoln. The cold war era was marked at Beale by the presence of B-52 bombers and the making of the movie *A Gathering of Eagles*, which was filmed at Beale in 1962. Cold war tension led to the development of the SR-71 Blackbird, which was stationed at Beale, and with the change to reconnaissance came the arrival of the U-2 Dragonlady. (Both, courtesy of Beale Air Force Base.)

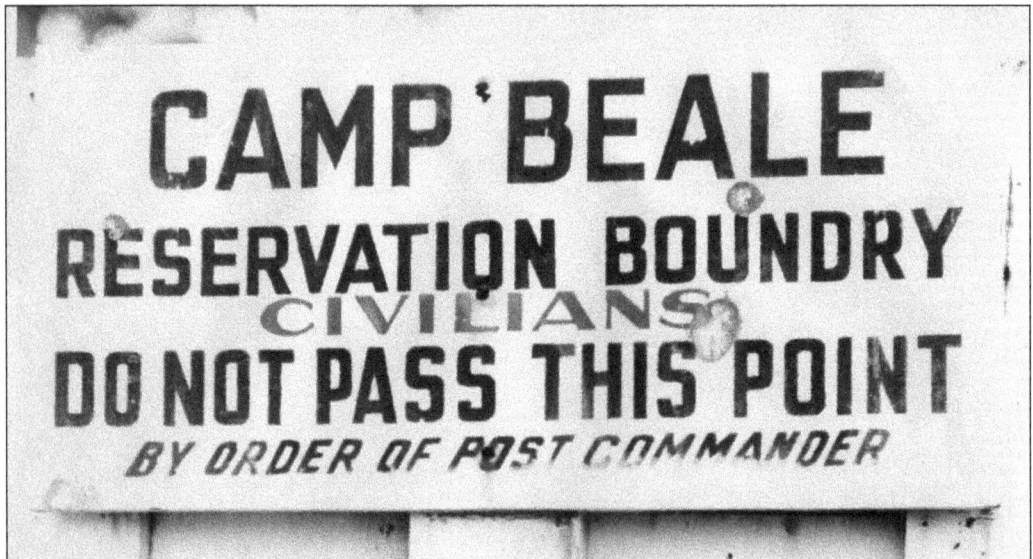

CAMP BEALE
RESERVATION BOUNDRY
CIVILIANS
DO NOT PASS THIS POINT
BY ORDER OF POST COMMANDER

This unexploded mortar shell was dug out of the ground in the Camp Far West area by Beale Explosive Ordnance soldiers. The bomb demonstrates the presence of military-related activities at Camp Beale during World War II. Bombs discovered by boys in Wheatland were used to play catch and to throw off the dam at Camp Far West. One bomb actually exploded, knocking a surprised young man over a hedge. (Courtesy of Richard Paskowitz.)

B-52 bombers, the workhorses of the air force, and KC-135 tankers fuel mid-air. During the cold war, B-52 bombers were based at Beale as part of the Strategic Air Command. These two giants were commonly seen in the skies over Wheatland. (Courtesy of Beale Air Force Base.)

The SR-71 Blackbird was based out of Beale Air Force Base and was used throughout the world in high-altitude, long-range surveillance. Many of the personnel involved with this remarkable aircraft retired in the Wheatland area. (Courtesy of Beale Air Force Base.)

A U-2 Dragonlady, based out of Beale Air Force Base, prominently hit the news when Francis Gary Powers was shot down over Russia in 1956. The U-2 was responsible for the aerial views of the Russian nuclear missile sites in Cuba in 1963. (Courtesy of Richard Paskowitz.)

116

Eight

IN THE BEGINNING

Much of the physical and visual history of the Wheatland area was lost throughout the years. Starting east with the 11,000-acre Spenceville Wildlife Refuge, the communities of Spenceville, Cabbage Patch (Waldo), and Round Tent are gone. Farther down the old Emigrant Trail, one came to Melon's Hotel, Milltown, McCourtney's Crossing, Graham's Hotel, past Camp Far West, down to Johnson's adobe house and to the Burtis Hotel before crossing the Bear River at Johnson's Crossing on the way to Sutter's Fort. All of these landmarks are gone. Kearney, a town laid out at Johnson's Crossing, never got off the drawing board. What does exist are some markers, collected and uncollected artifacts, old wagon wheel ruts in the land, depressions of Southern Maidu Indian homes and ceremonial sites, and some deteriorated structural foundations such as those found at the old Wire Bridge area near McCourtney's Crossing.

Farther west, to travel from Marysville to Sutter's Fort, one would probably have gone south down Oakley Lane and crossed Bear River at Kempton's Crossing where a hotel and a cemetery have long been buried under mining debris washed down from the Sierra foothills. Much of the land west of there was natural river-bottom silt land, treed and uncultivated until the late 1800s, when it was cleared, levees were built, and Reclamation District 817 was formed. In 1851, the town of Plumas City was conceived and, like Kearney, never materialized.

Like the hitching posts used to secure horses while their owners attended funerals at Lofton Cemetery, some physical and visual sights do remain today. On the site of the 1913 Durst hop farm riot, ghosts of the former hop drying kilns can still be seen from Spenceville Road just east of Wheatland. The old cannery, built when Prohibition was the law and hops were temporarily replaced by fruit trees, still stands at the site of the old town of Horstville. The first house in Wheatland, the Holland house, is still occupied, but the downtown area of Wheatland was destroyed by a series of fires, and no original buildings exist today.

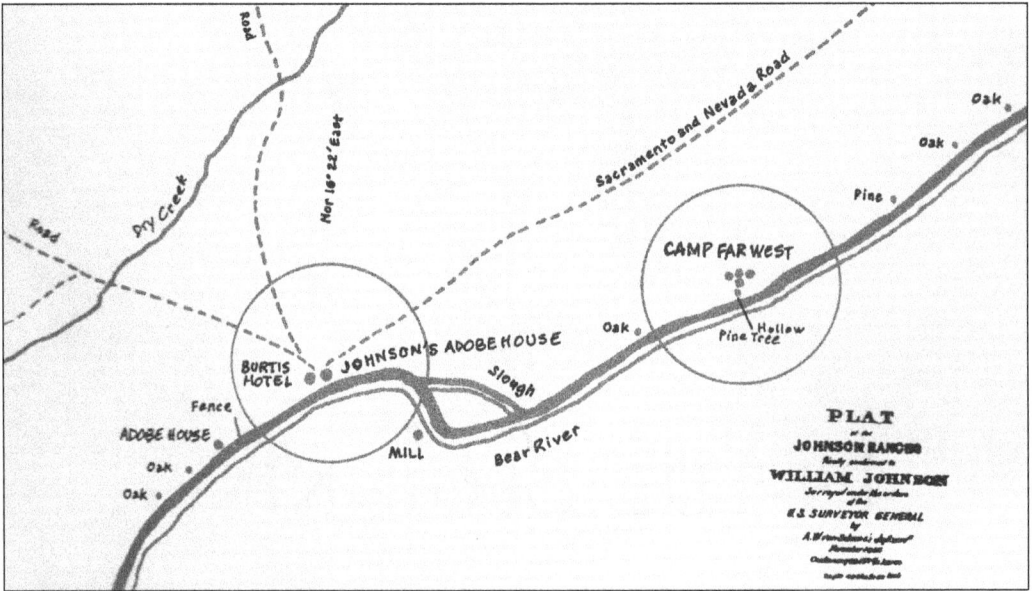

This early map (1849–1852) by the U.S. surveyor general shows Johnson's adobe house and the Burtis Hotel on Bear River. The Emigrant Trail came down the Sacramento-Nevada Road through Spenceville, Cabbage Patch, and Round Tent and crossed Bear River at Johnson's before heading on to Sutter's Fort. The oak and hollow pine trees were landmarks to help mark the trail. (Courtesy of Jack Steed.)

Two survey teams meet at McCourtney's Crossing around 1905. The tents belong to the U.S. government survey team. The men shown with the surrey are a crew surveying for building of a possible rail line near McCourtney's Crossing. (Courtesy of Wes Freeman.)

Taken in 1909, this picture is of the largest locally known oak tree before it fell in the late 1930s. Typical of the trees used for trail markers, it stood on property owned by the Durst Brothers. Pictured from left to right are (first row) Aurora Muck, Ethel Boswell, Rachail Hackett, Florence Jasper, Greta Jasper, and Ruby Jasper. The four men in the second row are unidentified. (Courtesy of the Aurora Muck Bowers family.)

This rock foundation is located at the Milltown site, a small community on Bear River below McCourtney's Crossing. John S. Moore built a sawmill in 1849 that was converted into a gristmill in 1854 by J. L. McDonald. In 1855, McDonald built a bridge above the mill, which washed away, and a wire suspension bridge was built in 1862. (Courtesy of Wes Freeman.)

The above photograph shows a depression marked by a flag. This depression contained the foundation of a ceremonial roundhouse or dance house that was used for Nisenan Indian ceremonies and special events in their village. A village consisted of extended families of 15 to 25 members, with up to 500 people living in large villages. These were semi-subterranean structures, dug down about 3 to 4 feet with heavy beams and two to four main posts supporting the tule, or earth-covered, roof. The Nisenan danced to celebrate the harvest, seasonal changes, birth, death, and the coming of manhood and womanhood. The rock, containing many shallow depressions (as shown in the photograph below), was reportedly used as a grinding area for processing food for ceremonial celebrations. (Both, courtesy of Wes Freeman.)

These Maidu Indian arrowheads, tools, mortars, and pestle are examples of the items found in the local area. Tools were made from basalt, soapstone, chalcedony, jasper, and obsidian. Stone knives, arrow points, club heads, scrapers, mortars, and pestles were efficient and effective in serving their purposes. Using stone or bone scrapers, women prepared animal hides for equipment bags, quivers, and clothing. Tule reeds made fine mats, boats, and roofing material. Milkweed and hemp fiber became either thread for sewing or rope for nets, snares, and sieves. All Nisenan girls learned to weave willow baskets, which were used for preparing, cooking, and storing food. There are numerous local sites once inhabited by Native Americans, and the locations of these sites were carefully documented and plotted using GPS coordinates. (Both, courtesy of Wes Freeman.)

This series of depressions, found near Dry Creek, was typical of areas used by the Native American women for food preparation. It was common to grind acorns into a rough textured mush. Pine nuts, grains, and grasshoppers were also ground for food. (Courtesy of Beale Air Force Base.)

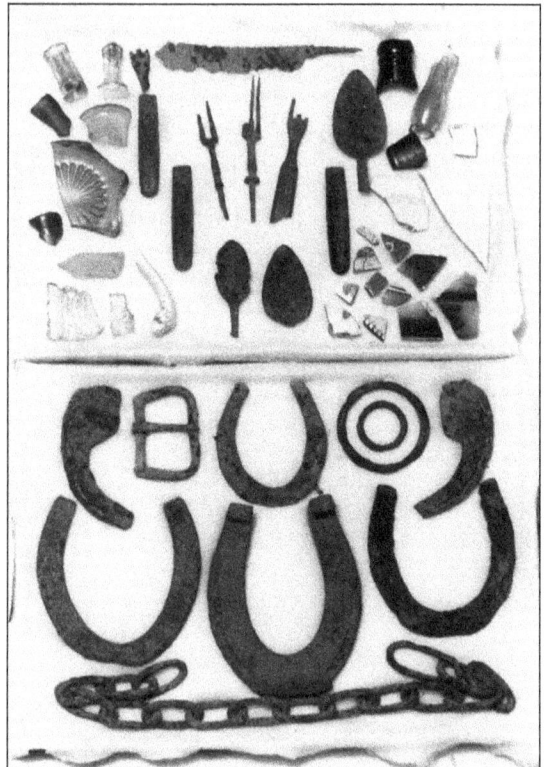

These artifacts were found at the sites of the Johnson adobe house and the Burtis Hotel by Richard and Jack Steed during their quest to identify the location of the structures. This discovery clearly identified the sites of the Johnson adobe house and the Burtis Hotel. They were able to identify and differentiate the two sites by the type and location of artifacts found. (Courtesy of Jack and Richard Steed.)

E. Clemens Horst Jr. stands next to this monument, placed at Johnson's Crossing in the spring of 1973 by the Wheatland Historical Society. The Horst family operated the hop farm at Horstville and in other California areas, as well as in Oregon and Washington. The plaque is on the site previously owned by the Horst family. The property was later purchased by the Damon estate and then by AKT Enterprises. (Courtesy of Maryl Liebra Parker.)

The Johnson's Ranch Historical Landmark No. 493 was placed by the California State Department of Parks and Recreation in cooperation with the Wheatland Lions Club in 1971. The plaque commemorates Johnson's rancho as being the first settlement reached by travelers on the Emigrant Trail, its history as an original part of the Pablo Gutierrez land grant, and as the site of Camp Far West. (Courtesy of Jack Steed.)

OVERLAND EMIGRANT TRAIL.

APPROXIMATELY 1 1/4 MILES EAST OF THIS SITE IS THE HISTORIC JOHNSON'S CROSSING. THIS WAS THE FIRST SETTLEMENT REACHED WEST OF THE SIERRA AND THE LAST STOP ON THE OVERLAND EMIGRANT TRAIL. USED AS A CAMPING SPOT FOR THE PIONEERS, DEPARTURE SPOT FOR THE MINERS AND A SOJOURNING PLACE FOR TRAPPERS HERDSMEN AND ADVENTURERS. THE RESCUE PARTY FOR THE DONNER PARTY WAS ORGANIZED AND DEPARTED FROM THIS CROSSING FEBRUARY 5, 1847.

CALIFORNIA REGISTERED HISTORICAL LANDMARK NO. 799-3

PLAQUE PLACED BY THE STATE DEPARTMENT OF PARKS AND RECREATION IN COOPERATION WITH THE YUBA COUNTY HISTORICAL SOCIETY, OCTOBER 23, 1976.

The Overland Emigrant Trail plaque on Spenceville Road is located one and a quarter miles northwest of Johnson's Crossing. Johnson's Crossing was the first settlement reached west of the Sierra and the last stop on the Overland Emigrant Trail. Johnson's Crossing was used by pioneers to camp, a place from which to depart for miners, and as a sojourning place for trappers, herdsmen, and adventurers. The rescue party for the Donner expedition was organized and departed from this crossing on February 5, 1847. (Courtesy of Jack Steed.)

Located between Kempton's Crossing and the railroad, the Bear River Bridge crossed the river where the road continued up Malone Avenue. Turning right onto Main Street, the road continued to downtown Wheatland onto Front Street and then back over the railroad tracks. The bridge, which no longer exists, made travel easier between Sheridan and Wheatland. (Courtesy of Elaine Phillips Tarke.)

Waldo Bridge, pictured above, crosses Dry Creek just northeast of the area called Cabbage Patch. Two enterprising black men settled here and grew cabbages in the boggy area along Dry Creek to provide food to the miners. In 1854, Abraham and Ellen Hambleton opened a hotel and a blacksmith shop. The Hambletons' graves are the only marked graves of the 17 at Waldo. Later the area became home to the Welch and Jones families. The bridge itself, built in 1901, is unique in that it is a Dundon Company bridge—a single-span, riveted, steel-truss bridge with a wooden plank deck. Dry Creek Bridge, pictured below, was east of Cabbage Patch, just downstream from Spenceville. Charles Lincoln Wilson Jr.'s survey party is shown crossing this early toll bridge in their surrey. (Above, courtesy of Rick and Jane Paskowitz; below, courtesy of Wes Freeman.)

Lofton Cemetery was the primary burial site for the residents of the Erle District. When much of Francis Lofton's descendants' land was confiscated by the government for Camp Beale, his granddaughter, Aphra (Harding) Gorton, was helped by Gov. Earl Warren to declare the Lofton family cemetery a state historical site. It was deeded to the state with the proviso that anyone of any race, creed, or color could be buried there free of charge. Camp Beale tried to cordon off the cemetery, but with the help of the Marysville sheriff, Aphra forced the base to reopen access to the cemetery, which contains more than 175 burial plots. The photograph above shows the old hitching posts once used to tie up horses and buggies. (Above, courtesy of Jamie Newman; below, courtesy of Ron Jauch.)

Kempton's Cemetery was located near Kempton's Crossing. Helen (Hudson) Stineman is pictured with the remains of one broken headstone. More than 100 people were buried here between 1850 and 1870. In 1874, the cemetery was finally completely buried underneath mining debris washed down from the foothills. It is periodically exposed after unusually high water in the Bear River washes away the sand and silt. (Courtesy of the Stineman family.)

Camp Far West Cemetery was used to bury soldiers and their families stationed at Cantonment Far West and travelers who died on the Emigrant Trail. The cemetery is on private property. With the wooden grave markers long gone, there are estimates that approximately 30 graves are there. A marker with four names was placed at the cemetery by the Native Daughters of the Golden West. (Courtesy of Jack Steed.)

Visit us at
arcadiapublishing.com

www.ingramcontent.com/pod-product-compliance
Lightning Source LLC
Chambersburg PA
CBHW050611110426
42813CB00008B/2526